Contents

KT-117-889

Get By in Spanish is divided into colour-coded topics to help you find what you need quickly. Each unit contains practical travel tips to help you get around and understand the country, and a **phrasemaker** to help you say what you need to and understand what you hear.

As well as listing key phrases, **Get By in Spanish** aims to help you understand how the language works so that you can start to communicate independently. The **check out** dialogues within each section show the language in action, and the **try it out** activities give you an opportunity to practise. The **link up** sections pick out the key structures and give helpful notes about their use. A round-up of all the basic grammar can be found in the **Language Builder**, pp132-138.

In Spanish, all nouns – things, people, concepts – are either masculine or feminine and this affects the way they are written and pronounced, and the words related to them. In the book these alternative endings are shown: masculine/feminine e.g. **amigo/a**, meaning male/female friend.

If you've bought the pack with the audio CD, you'll be able to listen to a selection of the most important phrases and **check out** dialogues, as well as all the **as if you were there** activities. You can use the book on its own, but the CD will help you to improve your pronunciation. A booklet containing the audioscripts is available to download from www.bbcactive.com/languages.

sounds Spanish

The written form and the spoken form of the Spanish language are very similar; each letter is usually pronounced in the same way each time you see it. It also helps that the pronunciation of many letters is very similar to the way you say them in English. This book uses a pronunciation guide, based on English sounds, to help you start speaking Spanish. Key points are also highlighted in the **sound checks** throughout the units.

vowels

	sounds like ...	shown as ...
a	'a' in 'man'	a
e	'e' in 'pen'	e/eh
i	'ee' in 'seem'	ee
o	'o' in 'hot'	o
u	'oo' in 'root'	oo
au	'ow' in 'owl'	ow

ei	'ay' in 'play'	ay
ie	'ye' in 'yes'	eeye
ue	'we' in 'went'	we
ua	'wa' in 'wag'	wa
ui	'wee' in 'weep'	wee

consonants

Although Spanish sounds are never exactly the same as their English equivalents, the following letters are very close.

	sounds like ...	shown as ...
b	b	b
d (except as a final letter)	d	d
f	f	f
k	k	k
l	l	l
m	m	m
n	n	n
p	p	p
s	s	s
t	t	t

These have quite a different pronunciation:

	sounds like ...	shown as ...
c + e/i	'th' in 'thin'	th
ch	'tch' in 'notch'	ch/tch
c + anything else	'k' in 'kit'	k
g + e/i	'ch' in Scottish 'loch'	*ch
g + anything else	'g' in 'go'	g
h	never pronounced	
j	'ch' in Scottish 'loch'	*ch
ll	'y' in 'yes'	y
ñ	'ni' in 'onion'	ny
q (always followed by u)	'k' in 'kit'	k
r (usually)	rolled	r
rr	strongly rolled	rr
v	'b' in 'bill'	b

w (very rare)	'v' in 'vat'	*v*
x (fairly rare)	's' in 'estimate'	*s*
y	'y' in 'yes'	*y*
z	'th' in 'thin'	*th*

variations

You will hear different pronunciations of some words throughout the Hispanic world. The key difference in the Spanish spoken in Southern Spain and in most of Latin America is in the pronunciation of the following letters: **ce**, **ci** and **z** sound like the 's' in 'sin', while **ll** and **y** sound like the 'j' in 'jam'.

stress

The part of a word stressed tends to follow different patterns in Spanish than in English. Stress is shown in this book in bold italics.

- If the word has a written accent, always put the stress on that part of the word:

  estación *estatheeon*

- If the word ends in a vowel, **-n** or **-s**, always stress the next to last syllable:

  oficina *ofeetheena*   correos *korreos*   cierran *theeyerran*

- If the word ends in a consonant other than **-n** or **-s**, always stress the last syllable:

  azul *athool*   total *total*   bañador *banyadoor*

alphabet

Here's a guide to how the Spanish pronounce the alphabet, which may be useful for spelling your name or an address.

A *ah*	B *beh*	C *theh*	D *deh*	E *eh*
F *efeh*	G **cheh*	H *atcheh*	I *ee*	J **chota*
K *ka*	L *eleh*	LL *ayeh*	M *emeh*	N *eneh*
Ñ *enyeh*	O *oh*	P *peh*	Q *koo*	R *erreh*
S *eseh*	T *teh*	U *oo*	V *oobeh*	W *oobeh dobleh*
X *ekees*	Y *eegreeyega*	Z *theta*		

Bare **Necessities**

phrasemaker

greetings
you may say ...

Hello!	¡Hola!	*o*la
Good morning.	Buenos días.	*bwe*nos *dee*as
Good afternoon/ evening.	Buenas tardes.	*bwe*nas *tar*des
Good evening/night.	Buenas noches.	*bwe*nas *no*tches
How are you?	¿Qué tal?	*keh* tal
Fine, thanks. How are you?	Muy bien, gracias. ¿Y usted?	*mooee bee***yen***, **gra**theeas ee oos**teh**
See you later.	Hasta luego.	*as*ta *lwe*go
See you tomorrow.	Hasta mañana.	*as*ta *manya*na
Bye!	¡Adiós!	*adee***yos**

other useful words
you may say ...

Excuse me.	¡Perdone!	*per**do**neh*
Sorry.	¡Perdón!	*per**don***
please	por favor	*por fa**bor***
Thank you (very much).	(Muchas) gracias.	*(**moo**tchas) **gra**theeas*
You're welcome.	De nada.	*deh **na**da*
Have a good trip!	¡Buen viaje!	*bwen **beea***cheh*
Have a nice meal!	¡Que aproveche!	*keh apro**be**tcheh*
Here you are.	Tenga.	*ten**ga***
okay	muy bien/vale	*mooee bee**yen**/**ba**leh*

It doesn't matter./ It's all right.	No importa.	*no eemporta*
Don't worry.	No se preocupe.	*no seh prayokoopeh*
Of course!	¡Claro!	*klaro*
yes/no	sí/no	*see/no*
sir/madam	Señor/Señora	*senyor/senyora*
Can I (come in)?	¿Se puede (pasar)?	*seh pwedeh (pasar)*

about yourself

you may say ...

My name is ...	Me llamo ...	*meh yamo*
I'm ...	Soy ...	*soy*
Mr ...	el señor ...	*el senyor*
Mrs ...	la señora ...	*la senyora*
Miss ...	la señorita ...	*la senyoreeta*
This is ...	Le presento ...	*leh presento*
Mr ...	al señor ...	*al senyor*
my husband.	a mi marido.	*a mee mareedo*
my colleague. (m/f)	a mi colega.	*a mee kolega*
my boyfriend.	a mi novio.	*a mee nobeeo*
This is ...	Le presento ...	*leh presento*
Mrs ...	a la señora ...	*a la senyora*
my wife.	a mi esposa.	*a mee esposa*
my girlfriend.	a mi novia.	*a mee nobeea*
I'm from ...	Soy de ...	*soy deh*
I'm ...	Soy ...	*soy*
Irish.	irlandés/irlandesa.	*eerlandes/eerlandesa*
(nationalities, p17)		
I live in ...	Vivo en ...	*beebo en*
I study economics.	Estudio económicas.	*estoodeeo ekonomeekas*
I'm a ...	Soy ...	*soy*
nurse.	enfermero/a.	*enfermero/a*
lawyer.	abogado/a.	*abogado/a*
I'm ...	Estoy ...	*estoy*
single.	soltero/a.	*soltero/a*
married.	casado/a.	*kasado/a*
divorced.	divorciado/a.	*deebortheeado/a*
widowed.	viudo/a.	*beeoodo/a*

I have three children.	Tengo tres hijos.	*tengo tres **ee***chos*
I'm 33 years old. (See numbers, p15)	Tengo treinta y tres años.	*tengo **trayn**ta ee tres anyos*
I speak a little Spanish.	Hablo un poco de español.	*ablo oon **po**ko deh espa**nyol***
I'm here on holiday/business.	Estoy aquí de vacaciones/negocios.	*es**toy** a**kee** deh baka**theeo**nes/ne**go**theeos*
I'm staying for a week.	Paso una semana aquí.	*paso **oo**na se**ma**na a**kee***
Do you speak English?	¿Habla usted inglés?	*abla oos**teh** een**gles***

check out 1

Another guest at your hotel starts chatting to you.

○ Hola. ¿Cómo se llama?
*ola. **ko**mo seh **ya**ma*

- Me llamo Sarah, ¿y usted?
*meh **ya**mo **sa**ra ee oos**teh***

○ Soy Alfonso. ¿De dónde es usted?
*soy al**fon**so. deh **don**deh es oos**teh***

- Soy de Londres, ¿y usted?
*soy deh **lon**dres ee oos**teh***

○ Soy mexicano.
*soy me***chee**kano*

Q What are you asked, apart from your name?
Where is Alfonso from?

¿Cómo se llama?	*komo seh yama*	What's your name?
Encantado/a.	*enkantado/a*	Nice to meet you.
¿De dónde es usted?	*deh dondeh es oosteh*	Where are you from?
¿Es usted inglés/ inglesa?	*es oosteh eengles/ eenglesa*	Are you English?
¿En qué trabaja?	*en keh traba*cha*	What do you do for a living?
¿Tiene hijos?	*teeyeneh ee*chos*	Do you have children?
¿Está usted aquí de vacaciones?	*esta oosteh akee deh bakatheeones*	Are you here on holiday?
¿Cuánto tiempo se queda?	*kwanto teeyempo seh keda*	How long are you staying for?
Yo también.	*yo tambeeyen*	So am I.

is/are there ...?

you may say ...

Is there a telephone?	¿Hay teléfono?	*aee telefono*
Are there any toilets?	¿Hay servicios?	*aee serbeetheeos*

where is/are ...?

you may say ...

Where's the station?	¿Dónde está la estación?	*dondeh esta la estatheeon*
Where are the shoes?	¿Dónde están los zapatos?	*dondeh estan los thapatos*
Where's the Hotel Castilla?	¿Dónde está el Hotel Castilla?	*dondeh esta el otel kasteeya*
It's ...	Está ...	*esta*
on the right.	a la derecha.	*a la deretcha*
on the left.	a la izquierda.	*a la eethkeeyerda*
at the end of the street.	al final de la calle.	*al feenal deh la kayeh*
100 metres away.	a cien metros.	*a theeyen metros*

do you have any ...?

you may say ...

Do you have any unleaded petrol?	¿Tiene gasolina sin plomo?	*teeyeneh gasoleena seen plomo*
Do you have any ... prawns?	¿Hay ... gambas?	*aee gambas*

you may hear ...

Sí, claro.	*see klaro*	Yes, of course.
Aquí tiene.	*akee teeyeneh*	Here you are.

how much ... ?

you may say ...

How much is that?	¿Cuánto es?	*kwanto es*
How much does it cost?	¿Cuánto vale?	*kwanto baleh*
How much are the ... a kilo? strawberries tomatoes	¿A cuánto están ... el kilo? las fresas los tomates	*a kwanto estan ... el keelo las fresas los tomates*
How much is that (altogether)?	¿Cuánto es (en total)?	*kwanto es (en total)*

I'd like ...

you may say ...

I'd like ... a shirt. a melon.	Quisiera ... una camisa. un melón.	*keeseeyera oona kameesa oon melon*
I'd like a kilo of oranges.	Déme un kilo de naranjas.	*demeh oon keelo deh naran*chas*

11

check out 2

You're shopping for tomatoes at the market.

○ Buenas tardes. ¿Hay tomates?
bwenas tardes. aee tomates

- Sí, claro.
see klaro

○ Déme dos kilos. ¿Cuánto es?
demeh dos keelos. kwanto es

- Un euro con sesenta.
oon eooro kon sesenta

○ Gracias, adiós.
gratheeas adeeyos

> **Q** Is it morning or afternoon?
> How much do you have to pay?

getting things straight
you may say ...

Pardon?	¿Cómo?	*komo*
Could you say that again?	¿Quiere repetir eso?	*keeyereh repeteer eso*
More slowly, please.	Más despacio, por favor.	*mas despatheeo por fabor*
I don't understand.	No entiendo.	*no enteeyendo*
Do you understand?	¿Entiende?	*enteeyendeh*

How do you write/ spell it? (See alphabet, p6)	¿Cómo se escribe?	*ko*mo seh es*kree*beh
Can you write it down, please?	¿Puede escribirlo, por favor?	*pwe*deh eskree*beer*lo por fa*bor*
What does it mean?	¿Qué quiere decir?	keh kee*yere*h de*theer*
I don't know.	No sé.	no seh
Is that right?	¿Verdad?	ber*da*

changing money

you may say ...

I'd like to change ... £50. $100.	Quiero cambiar ... cincuenta libras. cien dólares.	*keeye*ro kambee*ar* theen*kwen*ta *lee*bras *theeyen* *do*lares
What is the exchange rate?	¿A cómo está el cambio?	a *ko*mo es*ta* el *kam*beeo
What's the commission charge?	¿Cuánto es la comisión?	*kwan*to es la komee*seeon*
I've got traveller's cheques.	Tengo cheques de viaje.	*ten*go *che*kes deh bee*a**cheh

you may hear ...

¿Puedo ver su pasaporte?	*pwe*do ber soo pasa*por*teh	Can I see your passport?
La comisión es ...	la komee*seeon* es	The commission charge is ...
La libra está a un euro cuarenta y seis céntimos.	la *lee*bra es*ta* a oon *eoo*ro kwa*ren*ta ee *say*s *then*teemos	The pound is at €1.46.
un billete de veinte euros	oon bee*ye*teh deh *bayn*teh *e*ooros	a €20 note
una moneda de dos euros	*oo*na mo*ne*da deh dos *e*ooros	a €2 coin

check out 3

You want to change some pounds for euros.

- ○ Buenos días.
  bwenos deeas

- – ¿A cuánto está la libra?
  a kwanto esta la leebra

- ○ Está a un euro cuarenta y seis.
  esta a oon eooro kwarenta ee says

- – Quiero cambiar treinta libras.
  kyero kambeear traynta leebras

- ○ Vale. El pasaporte, por favor.
  baleh. el pasaporteh por fabor

Q What is the exchange rate?
What are you asked for?

the time

you may say …

What time is it?	¿Qué hora es?	*keh ora es*
What time do you open/close?	¿A qué hora abren/cierran?	*a keh ora abren/theeyerran*
What time does it leave/arrive?	¿A qué hora sale/llega?	*a keh ora saleh/yega*

14

Bare **Necessities**

you may hear ...

Es mediodía/ medianoche.	es medeeo**dee**a/ medeea**no**tcheh	It's midday/midnight.
Es la una.	es la **oo**na	It's one o'clock.
Son las dos/tres/ cuatro.	son las dos/tres/ **kwa**tro	It's two/three/four o'clock.
Son las diez y cinco de la mañana.	son las dee**yeth** ee **thee**nko deh la ma**nya**na	It's five past ten in the morning.
a las tres y cuarto de la tarde	a las tres ee **kwar**to deh la **tar**deh	at quarter past three in the afternoon
a las once menos cuarto de la noche	a las **on**theh **me**nos **kwar**to deh la **no**tcheh	at quarter to eleven at night
de las nueve menos veinte de la mañana	deh las **nwe**beh **me**nos **bayn**tch deh la ma**nya**na	from twenty to nine in the morning
hasta las siete y media de la tarde	**as**ta las see**ye**teh ee **me**deea deh la **tar**deh	until half past seven in the evening
dentro de ... diez minutos media hora	**den**tro deh dee**yeth** mee**noo**tos **me**deea **o**ra	in ... ten minutes half an hour

numbers

0	cero	**the**ro		12	doce	**do**theh
1	un/una, uno*	oon/**oo**na, **oo**no		13	trece	**tre**theh
2	dos	dos		14	catorce	ka**tor**theh
3	tres	tres		15	quince	**keen**theh
4	cuatro	**kwa**tro		16	dieciséis	deeyeth**ee**says
5	cinco	**theen**ko		17	diecisiete	deeyetheesee**ye**teh
6	seis	**say**s		18	dieciocho	deeyethee**o**tcho
7	siete	see**ye**teh		19	diecinueve	deeyethee**nwe**beh
8	ocho	**o**tcho		20	veinte	**bayn**teh
9	nueve	**nwe**beh		21	veintiuno	bayntee**oo**no
10	diez	dee**yeth**		22	veintidós	bayntee**dos**
11	once	**on**theh		23	veintitrés	bayntee**tres**

30	treinta	*traynta*		70	setenta	*setenta*
40	cuarenta	*kwarenta*		72	setenta y dos	*setentaeedos*
50	cincuenta	*theenkwenta*		80	ochenta	*otchenta*
51	cincuenta	*theenkwen-*		90	noventa	*nobenta*
	y uno	*taeeoono*		100	cien	*theeyen*
60	sesenta	*sesenta*		101	ciento uno	*theeyento oono*
65	sesenta y	*sesentaee*		103	ciento tres	*theeyento tres*
	cinco	*theenko*				

110	ciento diez	*theeyento deeyeth*
200	doscientos	*dostheeyentos*
293	doscientos	*dostheeyentos*
	noventa y tres	*nobenta ee tres*
300	trescientos	*trestheeyentos*
400	cuatrocientos	*kwatrotheeyentos*
500	quinientos	*keenyentos*
600	seiscientos	*saystheeyentos*
700	setecientos	*setetheeyentos*
800	ochocientos	*otchotheeyentos*
888	ochocientos	*otchotheeyentos*
	ochenta y ocho	*otchenta ee otcho*
900	novecientos	*nobetheeyentos*
1000	mil	*meel*
1047	mil cuarenta y siete	*meel kwarenta ee seeyeteh*
1590	mil quinientos noventa	*meel keeneeyentos nobenta*
2000	dos mil	*dos meel*
2380	dos mil trescientos	*dos meel trestheeyentos*
	ochenta	*otchenta*
3000	tres mil	*tres meel*
1,000,000	un millón	*oon meeyon*
1,675,834	un millón seiscientos	*oon meeyon saystheeyentos*
	setenta y cinco mil,	*setenta ee theenko meel*
	ochocientos treinta y	*otchotheeyentos traynta ee*
	cuatro	*kwatro*

(*el número uno = number one)

ordinal numbers

1st	primero/a	*preemero/a*
2nd	segundo/a	*segoondo/a*
3rd	tercero/a	*terthero/a*
4th	cuarto/a	*kwarto/a*
5th	quinto/a	*keento/a*
6th	sexto/a	*sesto/a*
7th	séptimo/a	*septeemo/a*
8th	octavo/a	*octabo/a*

countries & nationalities

Argentina: Argentinian	Argentina: argentino/a	*ar*chenteena: ar*chenteeno/a*
Australia: Australian	Australia: australiano/a	*owstraleeya: owstraleeyano/a*
Brazil: Brazilian	Brasil: brasileño/a	*braseel: braseelenyo/a*
Canada: Canadian	Canadá: canadiense	*kanada: kanadeeyenseh*
Chile: Chilean	Chile: chileno/a	*cheeleh: cheeleno/a*
England: English	Inglaterra: inglés/esa	*eenglaterra: eengles/esa*
(Northern) Ireland: Irish	Irlanda (del Norte): irlandés/esa	*eerlanda (del norteh): eerlandes/a*
Mexico: Mexican	México: mexicano/a	*me*cheeko: me*cheekano/a*
Morocco: Moroccan	Marruecos: marroquí	*marrwekos: marrokee*
New Zealand: New Zealander	Nueva Zelanda: neocelandés/esa	*nweba thelanda: nayothelandes/esa*
Scotland: Scottish	Escocia: escocés/esa	*eskotheea: eskothes/esa*
South Africa: South African	Sudáfrica: sudafricano/a	*soodafreeka: soodafreekano/a*
Spain: Spanish	España: español(a)	*espanya: espanyol(a)*
United States: American	los Estados Unidos: estadounidense, norte americano/a	*los estados ooneedos: estadooneedenseh norteh amereekano/a*
Wales: Welsh	Gales: galés/esa	*galles: galles/esa*

days

Monday	lunes	*loones*
Tuesday	martes	*martes*
Wednesday	miércoles	*meeyerkoles*
Thursday	jueves	**chwebes*
Friday	viernes	*beeyernes*
Saturday	sábado	*sabado*
Sunday	domingo	*domeengo*
today	hoy	*oy*
yesterday	ayer	*ayer*
the day before yesterday	anteayer	*anteeayer*
tomorrow	mañana	*manyana*
the day after tomorrow	pasado mañana	*pasado manyana*
last/next Thursday	el jueves pasado/ que viene	*el *chwebes pasado/ keh beeyeneh*
on Mondays	los lunes	*los loones*

months

January	enero	*enero*
February	febrero	*febrero*
March	marzo	*martho*
April	abril	*abreel*
May	mayo	*mayo*
June	junio	**chooneeo*
July	julio	**chooleeo*
August	agosto	*agosto*
September	se(p)tiembre	*se(p)teeyembreh*
October	octubre	*oktoobreh*
November	noviembre	*nobeeyembreh*
December	diciembre	*deetheeyembreh*

Bare **Necessities**

sound check

When **c** is followed by the letter **e** or **i** it is pronounced like the 'th' in 'thin'.

cebolla *the**bo**ya*   cinco *theenko*

Practise with these words:

cien *theeyen*   cincuenta *theen**kwe**nta*

catorce *ka**tor**theh*   doce *do**theh***

try it out

question time
What do you say when ...

1 you greet somebody in the afternoon?
2 you want to know what time a shop opens?
3 you want to introduce your wife?
4 you want to know where your hotel (the Hotel San Jorge) is?
5 you want somebody to repeat something?
6 you want to know if they have unleaded petrol?
7 you want to know how much to pay?
8 you need to find a toilet?

as if you were there
You're looking for a bank in Madrid, and stop a woman who's passing for help. Follow the prompts to play your part.

*(Say excuse me, then
say good morning)*
Buenos días.
(Ask where the bank is)
Al final de esta calle.

(Ask what time they close)
A las dos de la tarde.
(Thank her)
De nada, adiós.
(Say goodbye)

19

linkup

¿**Hay** servicios?	**Are there** any toilets?
¿**Tiene** helados?	**Do you have** ice creams?
Quiero cien gramos.	**I'd like** a hundred grammes.
Déme dos kilos.	**I'll have** two kilos.
¿**Dónde está** la estación?	**Where's** the station?
Soy inglés/inglesa.	**I'm** English.
Me llamo …	**My name is** …
Vivo en York.	**I live in** York.
Tengo dos hijos.	**I have** two children.

listening & replying

When people ask you questions about yourself, such as ¿Tiene hijos? (Do you have children?), it's tempting to reply using the same word: tiene.

But instead, you change the form of the word, and use tengo (I have) not tiene (you have):

Sí, tengo dos hijos. Yes, I have children.
No, no tengo hijos. No, I don't have children.

Some other common questions and possible replies:

¿Dónde vive? – Vivo en Southend. Where do you live? – I live in Southend.
¿Cómo se llama usted? – Me llamo David. What's your name? – My name is David.

Bare **Necessities**

missing words

Because the form of the verb tells you who is being referred to, it is very common not to use the words for 'I' (yo) or 'You' (usted) in Spanish:

Soy inglés. (not yo soy) I'm English.
Vivo en Southend. (not yo vivo) I live in Southend.
¿Tiene hijos? (not tiene usted) Do you have children?

The same applies to the words for he, she and it (él and ella):

¿Cómo se llama su hija? – Se llama Sara. (not Ella se llama Sara) What's your daughter called? – She's called Sara.
¿Dónde está el ascensor? – Está a la derecha. (not El está a la derecha) Where's the lift? – It's on the right.

the way you say things

You can't always transfer things word for word from one language to another. Me llamo David literally means 'Myself (I) call David'. So sometimes it pays to learn the whole phrase rather than the individual words.

Getting **Around**

arriving by air

International flights from most countries arrive at Madrid and Barcelona. There are also regular flights serving Alicante, Bilbao, Gran Canaria, Málaga, Palma de Mallorca, Santiago de Compostela, Seville, Tenerife, Valencia, Valladolid and Zaragoza. Charter flights go to other destinations, especially during high season. Wherever you fly to you will find it easy to catch onward bus or rail services to most towns, and taxis are usually a reasonably cheap option.

arriving by road

Madrid lies at the geographical centre of Spain and all major N (**Nacional**) roads start from there. Spain has invested heavily in new roads – especially along the Mediterranean coast and around Madrid – so it is worth getting an up-to-date road map. On some of the newest motorways (**autopistas**), you have to pay a toll (**peaje**).

car & bike hire

Hiring a car or bike in Spain can be up to 40% cheaper if you arrange it through a travel agent in your own country, so check out fly-drive options before you book your flight. Major car hire companies are represented at all main airports and train stations, but in tourist areas you may find smaller, independent operators much cheaper. You will need to show your passport and driving licence and must be over 21 with at least a year's experience. You can hire an under 75cc moped at 14, but you must be over 18 to hire anything bigger. Helmets are compulsory.

Spain has one of the highest accident rates in Europe, so take care. Drink driving, once a big problem, is now dealt with severely by the police. Parking, congestion and theft are a problem in larger cities, and watch out for wheel clampers and **la grua** (towaway crane); they involve a hefty fine and lots of paperwork.

road travel

Autopistas Fast two-, three- or four-lane motorways, often with a toll.

Autovías Much the same as autopistas, but without a toll.

N roads and Carreteras comarcales National main roads and local roads have two-way traffic, and sometimes speed limits and regulations to match autovías.

Speed limits 50km/h in built-up areas; 90km/h on roads outside built-up areas; 100km/h on dual carriageways and 120km/h on motorways. Remember seatbelts are compulsory. Hidden radar traps are common on main roads and police can demand large on-the-spot fines for speeding.

Petrol This is moderately priced, and most Spanish petrol stations accept credit cards. In remote areas, you may need to pay by cash.

Breakdowns see Emergencies, pp124-125.

rail travel

International rail routes from France go to San Sebastián and Madrid or to Barcelona, with onward connections to most other main cities. There are smaller border crossings through the Pyrenees to Cataluña and Aragón (often involving a change of train). From Portugal, main routes are from Lisbon to Madrid or from Porto to Galicia.

The main Spanish rail system is the state-run **RENFE**. Types of train include **cercanías** (local/commuter trains), **trenes regionales** (provincial trains) and the faster **trenes de largo recorrido** or **Electrotrén** (long-distance trains), which may be an **expreso** or the faster **rápido**. The fastest options are the **Intercity Talgo** or **Pendular trains**, though there are differing degrees of comfort, price and journey times, depending on the route and time you want to travel. The **Talgo** trains have air conditioning, music, sleeping carriages and TV.

A high-speed train, the **AVE**, links Madrid to Seville in under three hours. These more luxurious trains can cost up to 60% more. There are discounts available on certain days (**Días Azules**) and for groups. Smoking is banned on all Spanish public transport. For timetable information and to book online, visit: **www.renfe.es**.

tickets & passes

Buy your ticket at the ticket office or from automatic machines before you board your train, or you are liable for a fine. Children between four and eleven are eligible for a discount of 40%, depending on the route, and those under three travel for free.

Tarjeta Turística A first- or second-class rail pass available to any non-Spanish resident, which allows unlimited travel for three to ten days.

InterRail Pass Allows EU citizens under 26 unlimited travel for one month. Must also be bought in your own country.

Group discounts If travelling in a group of ten or more, you can get a 40% discount.

Senior citizens You are entitled to discount on Spanish trains if you obtain a REX card from your own country.

special trains

FEVE A conglomeration of small private companies that run a series of shorter routes not covered by **RENFE**, especially in out of the way tourist areas such as the north-western tip of Galicia and along the Cantabrian coast, from El Ferrol to Bilbao and Santander. This is a scenic route but services can be sporadic.

Expreso AlAndalus Operating from April to December, this is a five-day tour of the Andalusian cities of Seville, Córdoba, Granada, Málaga and Jerez de la Frontera. Tickets include meals and entertainment in exclusive restaurants and clubs in each city.

El tren de la naturaleza This scenic train runs from Cercedilla in the Madrid Sierra up a pine-forested mountain, with stops at villages and ski resorts.

El tren de la fresa A steam train that runs from Madrid to Aranjuez.

coaches & buses

Coaches often work out faster and no more expensive than local trains. Independent coach firms provide reasonably priced services all over Spain. **Autocares** (long-distance coaches) are quite fast, with air conditioning and videos. Buy your ticket at the office before boarding for longer journeys, or on the coach for shorter journeys.

Local buses are efficient and generally reliable, but check timetables carefully in rural or non-tourist areas, as there may be only one bus a day passing through. Sundays and **festivos** (holidays) may have extremely reduced services. You can buy an economical ten-trip card in an **estanco** (tobacconist's) or **quiosco** (newspaper kiosk). Free city bus route maps are available from tourist offices.

metro & cercanías services

You can buy metro tickets at the ticket office in each station, or from the automatic machine. Buy **un billete sencillo** for one journey or **un billete de diez** for ten single journeys. **Cercanías** (called **Rodalies** in Barcelona and Valencia) are commuter train networks that cover major metropolitan areas. Tickets can be bought at station ticket offices.

taxis

Taxis are relatively inexpensive, though you can be charged extra at night and on weekends and holidays. Each taxi driver should have a list of approved fares for trips to stations, airports and main sites.

ferries

International ferry connections link Bilbao and Santander with Britain. For the Balearic Islands there are ferry connections with Barcelona, Valencia and Denia.

phrasemaker

asking the way

you may say ...

Excuse me ...	Perdone, por favor ...	*perdoneh por fabor*
Which way is ...	¿ ..., por favor?	*... por fabor*
the market?	El mercado	*el merkado*
the (bus/train) station?	La estación (de autobuses/ del ferrocarril)	*la estatheeon (deh owtobooses/ del ferrokarreel)*
the town centre?	El centro (ciudad)	*el thentro (theeooda)*
Is ... near here?	¿Está por aquí ...	*esta por akee*
the cathedral	la catedral?	*la katedral*
the market	el mercado?	*el merkado*
the town hall	el Ayuntamiento?	*el aeeoontameeyento*
Is there ... near here?	¿Hay ... por aquí?	*aee ... por akee*
a bank	un banco	*oon banko*
a chemist's	una farmacia	*oona farmatheea*
an internet café	un cibercafé	*oon theeberkafeh*
a bus stop	una parada de autobús	*oona parada deh owtoboos*
Where is ...	¿Dónde está ...	*dondeh esta*
the main square?	la Plaza Mayor?	*la platha mayor*
St Martin's Church?	la iglesia de San Martín?	*la eegleseea deh san marteen*
the port?	el puerto?	*el pwerto*
I'm lost.	Estoy perdido/a.	*estoy perdeedo/a*

(See p59 for a list of shops, and pp104-105 for places to visit.)

you may hear ...

Allí está.	*ayee esta*	There it is.
a la derecha/a la izquierda	*a la deretcha/ a la eethkeeyerda*	to the right/to the left
todo recto	*todo rekto*	straight on

Getting **Around**

la ... a la derecha/ izquierda	la ... a la deretcha/ eethkeeyerda	the ... on the right/ left
primera	preemera	first
segunda	segoonda	second
tercera	terthera	third
Cruce el puente/ la calle/la plaza.	krootheh el pwenteh/ la kayeh/la platha	Cross the bridge/the street/the square.
en la esquina	en la eskeena	on the corner
a cien metros	a theeyen metros	100 metres away
al final de la calle	al feenal deh la kayeh	at the end of the street
(bastante) lejos	bastanteh le*chos	a (fairly) long way away
(muy) cerca	mooee therka	(very) close
¿Hay acceso para minusválidos?	aee aktheso para meenoosbaleedos	Is there disabled access?

check out 1

A passer by helps you find your way around.

○ ¿El castillo, por favor?
el kasteeyo por fabor

- Está al final de la calle, a la izquierda.
  esta al feenal deh la kayeh a la eethkeeyerda

○ Y ¿hay un cibercafé por aquí?
ee aee oon theeberkafeh por akee

- Sí, el café Cosmos, a quinientos metros.
  see el kafeh kosmos a keenyentos metros

Q Where is the castle?
The internet café is 15 metres away: true or false?

hiring a car or a bike
you may say ...

a hire car	un coche de alquiler	oon kotcheh deh alkeeler
I'd like to hire ...	Quisiera alquilar ...	keeseeyera alkeelar
a car.	un coche.	oon kotcheh
a motorbike.	una moto.	oona moto
a scooter.	una escúter.	oona eskooter
a bike.	una bicicleta.	oona beetheekleta
a ... car	un coche ...	oon kotcheh
small	pequeño	pekenyo
(fairly) big	(bastante) grande	(bastanteh) grandeh
three-door	de tres puertas	deh tres pwertas
for three days	para tres días	para tres deeas
Is insurance included?	¿Está incluido el seguro?	esta eenklooeedo el segooro
Unlimited mileage?	¿Kilometraje ilimitado?	keelometra*cheh eeleemeetado
How much is it?	¿Cuánto es?	kwanto es

Getting **Around**

you may hear ...

¿Qué tipo?	*keh **tee**po*	What type?
¿Para cuánto tiempo?	*para **kwan**to **teeyem**po*	For how long?
¿Quién conduce?	*kee**yen** kon**doo**theh*	Who will be driving?
Tenemos ...	*te**ne**mos*	We have ...
cincuenta euros al día/a la semana	*theen**kwen**ta e**oo**ros al **dee**a/a la se**ma**na*	€50 a day/a week
Su permiso de conducir/pasaporte, por favor.	*soo per**mee**so deh kondoo**theer**/pasa**por**teh por fa**bor***	Your driving licence/ passport, please.

check out 2

You want to hire a car for your holiday.

○ Quisiera alquilar un coche.
*keesee**yer**a alkee**lar** oon **ko**tcheh*

- ¿Qué tipo?
*keh **tee**po*

○ Un coche pequeño.
*oon **ko**tcheh pe**ke**nyo*

- Tenemos un coche de tres puertas a cincuenta euros al día, y uno de cinco puertas a sesenta euros.
*te**ne**mos oon **ko**tcheh deh tres **pwer**tas a theen**kwen**ta e**oo**ros al **dee**a ee **oo**no deh **theen**ko **pwer**tas a se**sen**ta e**oo**ros*

○ El de tres puertas, por favor.
*el deh tres **pwer**tas por fa**bor***

Q What kind of car do you want?
How much will you pay per day?

buying petrol

you may say ...

Is it self-service?	¿Es autoservicio?	*es owtoser**bee**theeo*
Where is ...	¿Dónde está ...	***don**deh esta*
the unleaded?	la sin plomo?	*la seen **plo**mo*
the diesel?	el diesel?	*el **deeye**sel*
the 4-star?	el Súper?	*el **soo**per*
Do you have ...	¿Tienen ...	***teeye**nen*
air?	aire?	***aee**reh*
water?	agua?	***a**gwa*
oil?	aceite?	*a**thay**eeteh*

you may hear ...

¿Algo más?	*algo mas*	Anything else?
número quatro	*noomero **kwa**tro*	(pump) number four

on the road

you may say ...

Is Cuenca far?	¿Está lejos Cuenca?	esta le*chos kwenka
How far is Cuenca? (See numbers p15)	¿A cuántos kilómetros está Cuenca?	a kwantos keelometros esta kwenka
How do you get to Almagro?	¿Por dónde se va a Almagro?	por dondeh seh ba a almagro
Is this the road to Segovia?	¿Es ésta la carretera de Segovia?	es esta la carretera deh segobeea
Where is Trujillo?	¿Dónde está Trujillo?	dondeh esta troo*cheeyo
Can I park here?	¿Puedo aparcar aquí?	pwedo aparkar akee
Where is the car park?	¿Dónde está el parking?	dondeh esta el parkeeng

check out 3

You stop for petrol and to ask directions.

○ Buenos días. ¿Dónde está la sin plomo?
  bwenos deeas. dondeh esta la seen plomo

- Allí. Número quatro.
  ayee. noomero kwatro

○ Gracias. ¿A cuántos kilómetros está Ávila?
  gratheeas. a kwantos keelometros esta abila

- A treinta kilómetros, más o menos.
  a traynta keelometros mas o menos

○ Gracias, adiós.
  gratheeas, adeeyos

Q What kind of petrol do you want?
How far is it to Avila?

travel by bus or metro

you may say ...

A single ticket, please.	Un billete sencillo.	*oon bee**ye**teh sen**thee**yo*
A ten-trip ticket, please.	¿Me da un billete de diez?	*meh da oon bee**ye**teh deh dee**yeth***
Does this train/bus go to Callao?	¿Va este tren/ autobús a Callao?	*ba **e**steh tren/ owto**boos** a ka**ya**o*
What number is it?	¿Qué número es?	*keh **noo**mero es*
What line is Sol on?	¿En qué línea está Sol?	*en keh **lee**nea esta sol*
Is the next stop Gracia?	¿La próxima parada es Gracia?	*la **pro**seema pa**ra**da es **gra**theea*
Does it stop at ...?	¿Para en ...?	*para en*

you may hear ...

la línea roja/negra	*la **lee**nea **ro***cha/ **ne**gra*	the red/black line
Cambie en ...	*kambeeyeh en*	Change at ...
El importe justo, por favor.	*el eem**por**teh ***choos**to por fa**bor***	Exact money, please.

taking a taxi

you may say ...

Is there a taxi rank?	¿Hay una parada de taxis?	*aee **oo**na pa**ra**da deh **ta**sees*
The airport/Hotel Pizarro, please.	Al aeropuerto/Hotel Pizarro, por favor.	*al ayero**pwer**to/o**tel** pee**tha**rro por fa**bor***
Is it far?	¿Está lejos?	*esta **le***chos*
Could I have a receipt?	¿Me da un recibo?	*meh da oon re**thee**bo*
How much is it?	¿Cuánto cuesta?	***kwan**to **kwes**ta*
Here you are.	Tenga.	***ten**ga*

32

you may hear ...

Está a media hora, más o menos.	*esta a medeea ora, mas o menos*	It's about half an hour away.
Está a unos tres kilómetros.	*esta a oonos tres keelometros*	It's about three kilometres away.

planning your journey
you may say ...

Are there buses/ trains to ...?	¿Hay autobuses/ trenes para ...?	*aee owtobooses/ trenes para*
What time does ... to Seville arrive/leave?	¿A qué hora llega/ sale ... para Sevilla?	*a keh ora yega/ saleh ... para sebeeya*
the bus	el autobús	*el owtoboos*
the train	el tren	*el tren*
the coach	el autocar	*el owtokar*
the ferry	el ferry	*el ferree*
What time does the next one leave? (See time, p14)	¿A qué hora sale el próximo?	*a keh ora saleh el proseemo*
Which platform does it leave from?	¿De qué vía sale?	*deh keh beea saleh*
Is there ...	¿Hay ...	*aee*
a lift?	ascensor?	*asthensor*
a left-luggage office?	consigna?	*konseegna*
How long does it take?	¿Cuánto tarda?	*kwanto tarda*
Is there a bar/ restaurant?	¿Hay bar/ restaurante?	*aee bar/restowranteh*
Do you have a timetable?	¿Tiene un horario?	*teeyeneh oon orareeo*

buying a ticket

you may say …

Where is the ticket office?	¿Dónde está la taquilla?	*dondeh esta la takeeya*
A return ticket for Burgos, please.	Un billete de ida y vuelta para Burgos, por favor.	*oon beeyeteh deh eeda ee bwelta para boorgos por fabor*
A single ticket, please.	Un billete de ida, por favor.	*oon beeyeteh deh eeda por fabor*
two adults and one child	dos adultos y un niño	*dos adooltos ee oon neenyo*
first/second class	primera/segunda clase	*preemera/segoonda klaseh*
I'd like to reserve … a seat. a couchette.	Quiero reservar … un asiento. una litera.	*keeyero reserbar oon aseeyento oona leetera*
Is there a reduction for … students? senior citizens?	¿Hay descuento para … estudiantes? pensionistas?	*aee deskwento para estoodeeantes penseeoneestas*

you may hear …

| Hay un suplemento de diez euros. | *aee oon sooplemento deh deeyeth eooros* | There's a €10 supplement. |

check out 4

You're at the station asking about trains to Toledo.

○ ¿Hay trenes para Toledo?
aee trenes para toledo

- Sí, a las once veinte y a las trece diez.
see a las ontheh baynteh ee a las tretheh deeyeth

○ ¿De qué vía salen?
deh keh beea salen

- Número nueve.
noomero nwebeh

○ ¿Cuánto tardan?
kwanto tardan

- Veinte minutos.
baynteh meenootos

○ Déme un billete de ida y vuelta.
demeh oon beeyeteh deh eeda ee bwelta

Q Trains to Toledo leave from platform three: true or false?
How long does the journey take?

sound check

q is always followed by **u** in Spanish and together they make a sound like the 'k' in 'kit'.

aquí *akee*   alquilar *alkeelar*

Practise with these words:

qué *keh*   pequeño *pekenyo*

quinientas *keeneeyentas*   izquierda *eethkeeyerda*

The **ll** sound in Spanish is very different from the 'l' in English. It is similar to the 'gh' sound in 'higher' and sounds almost like a 'y'.

billete *beeyeteh*   calle *kayeh*

Practise with these words:

castillo *kasteeyo*   taquilla *takeeya*

sencillo *sentheeyo*   muralla *mooraya*

try it out

picture this

Match each picture with the correct word or phrase.

a   a la izquierda   **d**   a las once y media

b   farmacia   **e**   servicios

c   un tren grande   **f**   a la derecha

crossed lines

These conversations have been mixed up. Rearrange the lines in the correct order.

1   Asking the way to the train station.

   a   La primera a la izquierda.

   b   Gracias.

   c   ¿Está lejos?

   d   ¿La estación del ferrocarril, por favor?

   e   No, a unos setecientos metros.

2   Asking about trains to Valencia.

   a   A las nueve treinta.

   b   Vía cinco.

   c   Gracias.

   d   ¿A qué hora sale el tren para Valencia?

   e   ¿De qué vía?

as if you were there

In the information office, you ask about getting to Salamanca. Follow the prompts to play your part.

Buenas tardes.

(Say good afternoon, and ask if there are buses to Salamanca)

Sí, hay autobuses y trenes.

(Ask when the bus leaves)

A las nueve, las once y las diecisiete.

(Ask how long it takes)

Dos horas y media.

(Ask for two return tickets)

linkup

key phrases

¿**Dónde está** la catedral?	**Where's** the cathedral?
¿**Está** lejos?	**Is it** far?
¿**Hay** un museo?	**Is there** a museum?
¿**Tiene** un plano de la ciudad?	**Do you have** a plan of the town?
Quisiera alquilar un coche.	**I'd like** to hire a car.
¿**A qué hora** abre?	**What time** does it open?

how to ask a question

Sometimes questions are easy because they follow the same pattern as in English:

¿Dónde está el banco? Where is the bank?
¿Cuánto es esto? How much is this?

But sometimes the word order is different:

¿Está cerca el banco? Is the bank nearby?
¿A qué hora sale el autobús? What time does the bus leave?

Notice that Spanish has no equivalent of the English use of 'do' or 'does' in questions.

For more on questions see the Language Builder, p136. ⋯⋯⟶

words for 'the' & 'a'

You've probably noticed that you say:

el banco (the bank) but **la** catedral (the cathedral)
un museo (a museum) but **una** iglesia (a church)

This is because in Spanish words for things are either masculine or feminine.
The word for 'the' is **el** for a singular masculine word and **la** for a singular feminine word.
The word for 'a' or 'an' is **un** for a masculine word and **una** for a feminine word.

For more on articles see the Language Builder, p132. ·····>

saying where things are

Two very useful expressions when you're touring:

Está lejos. It's a long way.
Está cerca. It's close.

When a place is near *to* or far *from* something, use **de**:

Está **cerca de** la Plaza Mayor. It's **close to** the main square.
Está **lejos de** la catedral. It's **far from** the cathedral.

When saying how far somewhere is in time or distance, use **a**:

Está **a** dos kilómetros. It's two kilometres **away**.
Está **a** diez minutos. It's ten minutes **away**.

Notice that the word for 'is' here is está, not es. Está is always used when referring to where something or someone is. Use están when talking about more than one thing or person.

For more on estar see the Language Builder, p138. ·····>

Somewhere **to Stay**

Spain has a wide range of accommodation available, from hotels and self-catering flats to remote farmhouses and old castles. Remember to book ahead for the hectic summer months when most coastal resorts will be packed. If you haven't booked ahead, you'll usually have to leave your passport as security until you have paid the bill. The Spanish tourist board can be a good place to start your search for accommodation: **www.spain. info**.

types of accommodation

Paradores Nacionales These are luxury state-run hotels in some of the most impressive beauty spots in Spain, often in converted historic buildings such as castles or monasteries. They are not cheap, but their inclusive packages can be extremely good value. See **www.parador.es** for details.

Hoteles These range from one to five stars. Once above three stars you can be sure of good-quality accommodation and facilities. By law, a price list must be displayed on the back of the bedroom door, and if you have any problems the hotelier must produce the **libro de reclamaciones** (complaints book).

Hostales Cheaper and more basic than hotels, these are graded from one to three stars. Even one-star **hostales** tend to offer a restaurant service.

Hostales Residenciales Much the same as **hostales**, but usually with a bar/café attached offering breakfast if required.

Pensiones and Casas de Huéspedes These tend to be more modest, family-run boarding houses. Meals can usually be requested.

Casas Rurales These traditional houses in rural areas offer the chance to really get away from it all. Horseriding, fishing and other outdoor activities are often available.

Campsites There are more than 800 official campsites, concentrated particularly on the coast, most with good facilities. Camping wild is permitted but check regulations locally or with tourist offices before pitching your tent. A list of sites can be found at **www.vayacamping.net**.

Albergues Juveniles Youth hostels are rarely cheaper than sharing a room in a cheap **pensión**. Most are found in the north, and require guests to show an HI card. See **www.reaj.com**.

Refugios These rudimentary huts in mountain areas are run for trekkers by the **Federación Española de Montañismo**. They offer basic kitchen facilities and bunk beds. See **www.fedme.es**.

Self-catering Eating out is cheap, so you won't necessarily save much by self-catering. However, having a whole villa or flat to yourselves can suit large families or groups.

children

Children of all ages are made very welcome in Spain. Most types of accommodation can provide cots and other facilities, but it is worth checking in advance if possible.

phrasemaker

finding a place
you may say …

Is there … near here? a hotel a campsite a flat to let	¿Hay … por aquí? un hotel un camping un apartamento de alquiler	*aee … por akee* *oon otel* *oon kampeeng* *oon apartmento deh* *alkeeler*
Do you have a room?	¿Tienen una habitación libre?	*teeyenen oona* *abeetatheeon leebreh*
a single/ double room	una habitación individual/ doble	*oona abeetatheeon* *eendeebeedwal/* *dobleh*
for … three people two adults and two children two nights a weekend a week	para … tres personas dos adultos y dos niños dos noches un fin de semana una semana	*para* *tres personas* *dos adooltos ee dos* *neenyos* *dos notches* *oon feen deh semana* *oona semana*
Can I see the room?	¿Puedo ver la habitación?	*pwedo ber la* *abeetatheeon*
How much is the room?	¿Cuánto cuesta la habitación?	*kwanto kwesta la* *abeetatheeon*
Do you have anything cheaper?	¿Tiene algo más barato?	*teeyeneh algo mas* *barato*
Is there … a reduction for children? a single supplement?	¿Hay … descuento para niños? suplemento individual?	*aee* *deskwento para* *neenyos* *sooplemento* *eendeebeedwal*
We'll see.	Ya veremos.	*ya beremos*
We'll take it.	La tomamos.	*la tomamos*

Somewhere **to Stay**

you may hear ...

¿Para cuántas ... noches? personas?	*para kwantas notches personas*	How many ... nights? people?
Lo siento. Está todo completo.	*lo syento. esta todo kompleto*	I'm sorry. We're full.
Los niños a mitad de precio.	*los neenyos a meetath deh pretheeo*	Children half-price.
impuestos incluidos	*eempwestos eenklweedos*	all taxes included

check out 1
You're at the hotel reception asking about a room.

○ Buenas tardes.
bwenas tardes

- Buenas tardes. ¿Tienen una habitación libre?
bwenas tardes. teeyenen oona abeetatheeon leebreh

○ ¿Una habitación doble?
oona abeetatheeon dobleh

- Sí, doble.
see dobleh

○ ¿Para cuántas noches?
para kwantas notches

- Una noche.
oona notcheh

○ Vale.
baleh

- ¿Cuánto cuesta?
kwanto kwesta

○ Ochenta y cinco euros la habitación.
otchenta ee theenko eooros la abeetatheeon

Q You want a single room: true or false?
How many nights do you want to stay?

specifications & services

you may say …

Does it have …	¿Tiene …	*teeye*neh
a bathroom?	baño?	*ban*yo
a shower?	ducha?	*doo*tcha
a cot?	cama de niño?	*ka*ma deh *nee*nyo
a sink?	lavabo?	la*ba*bo
a window?	ventana?	ben*ta*na
with a … bed	con cama …	kon *ka*ma
single	individual	eendeebee*dwal*
double	de matrimonio	deh matree*mo*neeo
with two beds	con dos camas	kon dos *ka*mas
Is breakfast included?	¿Está incluido el desayuno?	esta een*klwee*do el desa*yoo*no
How much is …	¿Cuánto es …	*kwan*to es
full board?	la pensión completa?	la pen*seeon* com*ple*ta
half board?	la media pensión?	la *me*deea pen*seeon*
Do you have a room on the ground floor?	¿Tiene habitación en la planta baja?	*teeye*neh abeeta*theeon* en la *plan*ta ba*cha
Is the bathroom wheelchair-friendly?	¿Está adaptado el cuarto de baño para sillas de rueda?	esta adap*ta*do el *kwar*to deh *ban*yo *pa*ra *see*yas deh *rwe*da

you may hear …

El desayuno es aparte.	el desa*yoo*no es a*par*teh	Breakfast is separate.
No tenemos camas de matrimonio.	no te*ne*mos *ka*mas deh matree*mo*neeo	We don't have any double beds.

Somewhere to Stay

checking in

you may say ...

I have a reservation.	Tengo una reserva.	*tengo oona reserba*
in the name of ...	a nombre de ...	*a nombreh deh*
Where can I park?	¿Dónde puedo aparcar?	*dondeh pwedo aparkar*
What floor is it on?	¿En qué piso está?	*en keh peeso esta*
Where's ...	¿Dónde está ...	*dondeh esta*
the lift?	el ascensor?	*el asthensor*
the staircase?	la escalera?	*la eskalera*
the restaurant?	el restaurante?	*el restowranteh*
What time is ...	¿A qué hora es ...	*a keh ora es*
breakfast?	el desayuno?	*el desayoono*
dinner?	la cena?	*la thena*
Is there ...	¿Hay ...	*aee*
air conditioning?	aire acondicionado?	*aeereh akondeetheeonado*
internet?	internet?	*eenternet*
room service?	servicio de habitaciones?	*serbeetheeo deh abeetatheeones*

you may hear ...

El nombre/El pasaporte, por favor.	*el nombreh/ el pasaporteh por fabor*	Your name/Your passport, please.
¿Quiere rellenar la ficha?	*keeyereh reyenar la feetcha por fabor*	Please fill in the form.
Es el número veintiuno.	*es el noomero baynteeoono*	It's room number 21.
Está en el tercer piso.	*esta en el terther peeso*	It's on the third floor.
a la derecha/ izquierda	*a la deretcha/ eethkeeyerda*	on the right/ left
Desde las siete y media hasta las diez.	*desdeh las seeyeteh ee medeea asta las deeyeth*	From 7.30 to 10.00. (See time, p14)
Aquí tiene la llave.	*akee teeyeneh la yabeh*	Here's the key.

check out 2

You're checking into a hotel with a reservation.

○ Tengo una reserva a nombre de Rodríguez.
  tengo oona reserba a nombreh deh rodreegeth

- Vale. Un momento por favor … sí, Rodríguez, una habitación individual para dos noches.
  baleh. oon momento por fabor … see rodreegeth oona abeetatheeon eendeebeedwal para dos notches

○ ¿Está incluido el desayuno?
  esta eenklweedo el desayoono

- No, el desayuno cuesta nueve euros.
  no el desayoono kwesta nwebeh eooros

○ Vale.
  baleh

- El pasaporte, por favor. Y ¿quiere rellenar esta ficha?
  el pasaporteh por fabor. ee keeyereh reyenar esta feetcha

Q Breakfast is included: true or false?
What two things are you asked?

asking for help

you may say ...

Could you call me at eight?	¿Pueden llamarme a las ocho?	*pweden yamarmeh a las otcho*
Do you have ... a safe? a map of the town?	¿Tienen ... una caja fuerte? un plano de la ciudad?	*teeyenen oona ka*cha fwerteh oon plano deh la theeooda*
Can you order me a taxi?	¿Me puede pedir un taxi?	*meh pwedeh pedeer oon tasi*
Can I have another towel?	¿Me hace el favor de darme otra toalla?	*meh atheh el fabor deh darmeh otra toaya*
... isn't working. The television The telephone The light switch	... no funciona. La televisión El teléfono El interruptor de la luz	*... no foontheeona la telebeeseeon el telefono el eenterrooptor deh la looth*
There's no ... hot water. toilet paper.	No hay ... agua caliente. papel higiénico.	*no aee agwa kaleeyenteh papel ee*cheeyeneeko*
There are no ... pillows. blankets. hangers.	No hay ... almohadas. mantas. perchas.	*no aee almoadas mantas pertchas*
How does ... work? the blind the shower the lock	¿Cómo funciona ... la persiana? la ducha? la cerradura?	*komo foontheeona la perseeana la dootcha la therradoora*
Do you have an iron?	¿Tienen una plancha?	*teeyenen oona plantcha*
The room is very ... noisy. cold. hot.	En mi habitación ... hay mucho ruido. hace mucho frío. hace calor.	*en mee abeethatheeon aee mootcho rweedo atheh mootcho freeo atheh mootcho kalor*

Ahora viene alguien.	*aora beeyeneh algeeyen*	There's somebody coming along now.
Las traigo ahora.	*las traeego aora*	I'll get you some.
Se aprieta este botón.	*seh apreeyeta esteh boton*	You press this button.

check out 3

You're having some problems with your hotel room.

○ Por favor, ¿cómo funciona la televisión?
  por fabor komo foontheeona la telebeeseeon

- Se aprieta este botón. (He shows you)
  seh apreeyeta esteh boton

○ Gracias. Y no hay agua caliente en el cuarto de baño.
  gratheeas. ee no aee agwa kaleeyenteh en el kwarto deh banyo

- No, hay un problema con el agua. Ahora viene alguien.
  no aee oon problema kon el agwa. aora beeyeneh algeeyen

○ Gracias.
  gratheeas

- De nada.
  deh nada

Q What two problems do you have?

checking out

I'd like to pay the bill …	Quiero pagar la cuenta …	*keeyero pagar la kwenta*
by credit card.	con tarjeta de crédito.	*kon tar*cheta deh kredeeto*
with cash.	en metálico.	*en metaleeko*

I think there's a mistake.	Creo que hay un error.	*krayo keh aee oon error*

you may hear …

¿Qué número de habitación?	*keh noomero deh abeetatheeon*	What room number?
La llave, por favor.	*la yabeh por fabor*	The key, please.
¿Cómo va a pagar?	*komo ba a pagar*	How will you pay?
Firme aquí.	*feermeh akee*	Sign here, please.

check out 4

It's time to settle your bill.

○ Quiero pagar la cuenta.
keeyero pagar la kwenta

- Vale. ¿Qué número de habitación tiene?
baleh. keh noomero deh abeetatheeon teeyeneh

○ La cuatrocientos setenta y siete.
la kwatrotheeyentos setenta ee seeyeteh

- Pues son ciento dieciocho euros, todo incluido. ¿Cómo va a pagar?
pwes son theeyento deeyeth ee otcho eooros todo eenklweedo. komo ba a pagar

○ Con tarjeta de crédito.
kon tar*cheta deh kredeeto

○ Vale. ¿Quiere firmar aquí? Gracias. Adiós y ¡buen viaje!
baleh. keeyereh feermar akee. gratheeas. adeeyos ee bwen beea*cheh

Q The bill is less than €120: true or false? How do you pay?

campsites

you may say ...

Do you have space for ...	¿Tienen sitio para ...	*teeyenen seeteeo para*
a car?	un coche?	*oon kotcheh*
a motorbike?	una moto?	*oona moto*
a caravan?	una caravana?	*oona karabana*
a tent?	una tienda?	*oona teeyenda*
How much is it?	¿Cuánto cuesta?	*kwanto kwesta*
Where are ...	¿Dónde están	*dondeh estan*
the showers?	las duchas?	*las dootchas*
the dustbins?	los cubos de la basura?	*los koobos deh la basoora*
the toilets?	los servicios?	*los serbeetheeos*
Where is ...	¿Dónde está ...	*dondeh esta*
the electricity?	la corriente?	*la korreeyenteh*
the drinking water?	el agua potable?	*el agwa potableh*
Is there ...	¿Hay ...	*aee*
a shop?	tienda?	*teeyenda*
a laundry?	lavandería?	*labandereeya*
a swimming pool?	piscina?	*peestheena*

you may hear ...

La caravana cuesta ... euros al día.	*la karabana kwesta ... eooros al deea*	The caravan costs ... euros a day.

Somewhere to Stay

self-catering and youth hostels

you may say ...

I'd like to rent ... the flat. the house.	Quiero alquilar ... el apartamento. la casa.	*keeyero alkeelar el apartamento la kasa*
When are the dustbins emptied?	¿Cuándo se vacían los cubos de la basura?	*kwando seh batheeyan los koobos deh la basoora*
Do we have to sort the waste (for recycling)?	¿Hay que separar cada tipo de basura (para reciclarla)?	*aee keh separar kada teepo deh basoora (para retheeklarla)*
Are there any additional costs?	¿Hay gastos adicionales?	*aee gastos adeetheeonales*
How does the ... work? heating cooker	¿Cómo funciona ... la calefacción? la cocina?	*komo foontheeona la kaleefaktheeon la kotheena*
Is the villa/hostel suitable for a wheelchair?	¿Está adaptado el chalet/el hostal para sillas de ruedas?	*esta adaptado el shaleh/el ostal para seeyas deh rwedas*
Can I hire ... a sleeping bag? some sheets?	¿Puedo alquilar ... un saco de dormir? sábanas?	*pwedo alkeelar oon sako deh dormeer sabanas*
What time do you lock up?	¿A qué hora cierran?	*a keh ora theeyerran*

you may hear ...

Funciona así.	*foontheeona asee*	It works like this.
Hay contador para la electricidad.	*aee kontador para la elektreetheeda*	There's a meter for the electricity.
temporada alta/baja	*temporada alta/ba*cha*	high/low season
Puede dejar la llave con un vecino.	*pwedeh de*char la yabeh kon oon betheeno*	You can leave the key with a neighbour.

b and **v** are pronounced in the same way, like the 'b' in 'bill'.
va *ba*   baño *banyo*

Practise with these words:
viene *beeyeneh*   habitación *abeetatheeon*
nombre ***nom**breh*   ver *ber*
veinte ***bayn**teh*   buen *bwen*

try it out

all the 'a's
Only the letter a remains in these words. Use the clues to fill them in.

1 - a - - - a - - - - a place to sleep
2 - - - - - - a … and a way to make sure you get one
3 - - a - - necessary to get into your room
4 - a - a sweet dreams on this!
5 - a - a - - - - - you may have to show this to check in
6 a - - - - - - - an easy way of getting to the top floor
7 - - - a - - - a … and another, not quite so easy
8 - - - - a - - a - - - the place where you go to eat
9 - - - a - - - - the first meal of the day
10 - - - a … and the last
11 - - - - a something you freshen up in
12 a - - a and what comes out of it

Somewhere to Stay

in the mix

The different parts of this conversation have got mixed up. Try to put them in the correct order.

a Muchas gracias.
b Sí, aquí a la derecha.
c Sí. ¿Cuánto es?
d Son ochenta y ocho euros la habitación.
e De nada. Hasta luego.
f No, el desayuno es aparte, a ocho euros por persona.
g Vale. La tomamos.
h Desde las siete de la mañana hasta las diez.
i Gracias. ¿Hay ascensor?
j Sí ... ¿una habitación doble?
k Ah, y ¿a qué hora es el desayuno?
l Es la habitación número quinientos treinta y cuatro. Aquí tiene la llave.
m Buenas tardes. ¿Tienen una habitación libre para una noche?
n ¿Desayuno incluido?

as if you were there

You're at the hotel reception ready to check out. Follow the prompts to play your part.

Buenos días.
(Greet the receptionist, and say you want to pay your bill)
Muy bien. ¿Qué número de habitación tiene?
(Say 47)
¿Cómo va a pagar?
(Say by credit card)
Muy bien. ¿Quiere firmar aquí?
(Say thanks and goodbye)

linkup

¿**Tienen** una habitación doble?	**Do you have** a double room?
¿**Hay** ascensor?	**Is there** a lift?
¿**Dónde está** el restaurante?	**Where's** the restaurant?
No hay aire acondicionado.	**There isn't** any air conditioning.
La televisión **no funciona**.	The television **doesn't work**.

describing things

When you say 'The hotel is very big' in Spanish, the words come in the same order as in English:

El hotel es muy grande. The hotel is very big.

But if you say 'a big hotel', the word order changes:

un hotel grande a big hotel

Some more examples:

una cama individual a single bed
una habitación doble a double room

One or two exceptions to this practice:

el primer piso the first floor
el segundo plato the second course

The words grande, doble, individual are known as adjectives or describing words.

Many adjectives in Spanish end in **-o** or **-a**. Just as the words for 'a' and 'the' change according to the gender of the word they describe, so too do adjectives ending in **-o** or **-a**:

un hotel modern**o** a modern hotel (hotel is masculine, so you use the masculine form of modern**o**, ending **-o**)
una cama cómod**a** a comfortable bed (cama is feminine, so cómod**a** has its feminine ending **-a**)

Adjectives ending in **-e** are the same for both masculine and feminine words:

un hotel grande a big hotel
una habitación grande a big room

For more on adjectives, see the Language Builder, p135.······⟩

saying 'no': negatives

The word no means 'no':

¿Tienen una habitación individual? – No, lo siento.
Do you have a single room? – No, I'm sorry.

But it also means 'not', 'isn't' or 'doesn't':

No hay aire acondicionado. There isn't any air conditioning.
El ascensor no funciona. The lift doesn't work.

Buying **Things**

opening hours

Shops are generally open from 9 or 10am until 2pm, and from 5pm until 8pm on weekdays. Most close at 2pm on Saturday and all day Sunday, though you will normally find somewhere in each neighbourhood to buy basics such as bread, drinks and snacks. Larger supermarkets, hypermarkets, chain stores and smaller shops in tourist areas stay open all day, often until 10pm Banks open from 8.30am to 2.30pm on weekdays, and from 8am till midday on Saturdays.

department stores

El Corte Inglés is a department store with branches in every decent-sized town, where you can buy everything from food and jewellery to camping gear, and do everything from booking excursions or seats for a concert or the theatre, to having your hair done. Larger shops and supermarkets accept major credit cards.

souvenirs

Shoes and leather goods These are relatively cheap, and it is easy to find well-made, elegant or original designs. Get bargains around Alicante and in the Balearic islands, Spain's shoe-producing centres.

Ceramics and azulejos (floor and wall tiles) The most traditional come from Talavera de la Reina in La Mancha and Manises, near Valencia, but they are sold all over Spain. Each locality has its own special designs.

Wine, cava and liqueurs These are all good value. You can buy most local specialities such as **jerez** (sherry) and **cava** (Spanish champagne) all over Spain. Wines with a good reputation, such as Rioja, Riberas del Duero and Rueda are also easy to buy, and less well-known wines such as Requena also offer good value.

Olive oil A true delicacy that can be pricey, but worth treating yourself to a good bottle for salads. The higher the **acidez** (acidity) (0.7%/0.9%) the stronger, richer and more distinctive the flavour.

Handwoven rugs Colourful and cheap. Try most outdoor markets and craft stores, especially those in Cáceres, Granada or Murcia.

Silver goods These are renowned in and around Córdoba, though you can find bargains elsewhere.

Metalwork Knives, swords and sabres crafted in black steel and inlaid with intricate gold leaf are a particular speciality of Toledo. Smaller gifts such as earrings and pendants are also available and sold in other parts of Spain.

Wickerwork This craft is especially developed in Tenerife.

Lace Look out for local designs of handmade lace.

food markets

If you are self-catering, your best bet for buying good-value fresh food is the local central market; often surrounded by busy greengrocers and delicatessens. Look out for **jamón serrano** (cured ham) **chorizo** (sausage) and cheeses such as **queso manchego** (cheese from La Mancha). For other specialities, see Eating Out, pp83–95.

Boquería, Barcelona A bustling and colourful daily food market, worth a visit for its atmosphere and its excellent fresh produce.

Mercado Central, Valencia A morning food market in a huge building, said to be one of the largest markets in Europe.

El Rastro, Madrid A weekly flea market, ideal for picking up bargain clothes and souvenirs.

phrasemaker

general phrases

you may say ...

Do you have any ...	¿Tiene ...	*teeyeneh*
olive oil?	aceite de oliva?	*athayeeteh de oleeba*
gloves?	guantes?	*gwantes*
sausage?	chorizo?	*tchoreetho*
orange juice?	zumo de naranja?	*thoomo deh naran*cha*
milk?	leche?	*letcheh*
How much is it/are they?	¿Cuánto es/son?	*kwanto es/son*
How much are ...	¿A cuánto están ...	*a kwanto estan*
the bananas?	los plátanos?	*los platanos*
the plums?	las ciruelas?	*las theerwelas*
I'll have ... please.	Déme ...	*demeh*
two kilos	dos kilos.	*dos keelos*
a hundred grammes	cien gramos.	*theeyen gramos*
Can I try some?	¿Puedo probar?	*pwedo probar*
this one/that one	éste/aquél	*esteh/akel*
these/those	estos/aquéllos	*estos/akeyos*
How much is it (altogether)?	¿Cuánto es (en total)?	*kwanto es (en total)*
Nothing else, thanks.	Nada más, gracias.	*nada mas, gratheeas*

you may hear ...

¿En qué puedo servirle?	*en keh pwedo serbeerleh*	Can I help you?
¿Qué desea?	*keh desea*	What would you like?
¿Cuánto/Cuánta quiere?	*kwanto/kwanta keeyereh*	How much would you like?
¿Cuántos/Cuántas quiere?	*kwantos/kwantas keeyereh*	How many would you like?
¿Algo más?	*algo mas*	Anything else?

Buying **Things**

Lo siento, no tenemos./No, no hay.	*lo seeyento no tenemos/no no aee*	I'm sorry, we don't have any.
Aquí tiene.	*akee teeyeneh*	Here you are.
Son siete euros ochenta.	*son seeyeteh eooros otchenta*	That's €7.80.
abierto/cerrado	*abeeyerto/therrado*	open/closed

shops

baker's	la panadería	*la panadereea*
cake shop	la pastelería	*la pastelereea*
butcher's	la carnicería	*la karneethereea*
chemist's	la farmacia	*la farmatheea*
delicatessen	la charcutería	*la charkootereea*
department store	los grandes almacenes	*los grandes almathenes*
flea market	el mercadillo	*el merkadeeyo*
general food store	tienda de comestibles/ alimentación	*teeyenda deh komesteebles/ aleementatheeon*
greengrocer's	la verdulería	*la berdoolereea*
fruiterer's	la frutería	*la frootereea*
jeweller's	la joyería	*la *choyereea*
market	el mercado	*el merkado*
newspaper stand	el quiosco	*el keeosko*
Post Office	Correos	*korrayos*
shoe shop	la zapatería	*la thapatereea*
shop	la tienda	*la teeyenda*
shopping centre	el centro comercial	*el thentro komertheeal*
stationer's	la papelería	*la papelereea*
supermarket	el supermercado	*el soopermerkado*
tobacconist's	el estanco	*el estanko*
travel agent's	la agencia de viajes	*la a*chentheea deh beea*ches*
watchmaker's	la relojería	*la relo*chereea*

quantities

you may say ...

a litre/kilo	un litro/kilo	*oon leetro/keelo*
half a litre/kilo	medio litro/kilo	*medeeo leetro/keelo*

100 grammes of
  boiled ham
  cured ham
	cien gramos de
	  jamón de York
	  jamón serrano
		*theeyen gramos deh
		  *chamon deh York
		  chamon serrano

250 grammes/ a quarter of a kilo	doscientos cincuenta gramos/un cuarto de kilo	*dostheeyentos theenkwenta gramos/ oon kwarto deh keelo*
a bag	una bolsa	*oona bolsa*
a bit more/less	un poco más/menos	*oon poko mas/menos*
a little bit (of cheese)	un poquito (de queso)	*oon pokeeto (deh keso)*
a bottle (of olive oil)	una botella (de aceite de oliva)	*oona boteya (deh athayeeteh deh oleeba)*
a dozen (eggs)	una docena (de huevos)	*oona dothena (deh webos)*
a packet (of butter)	un paquete (de mantequilla)	*oon paketeh (deh mantekeeya)*
a tin (of sardines)	una lata (de sardinas)	*oona lata (deh sardeenas)*
a piece/slice (of cake)	un pedazo (de pastel)	*oon pedatho (deh pastel)*
Can I have another?	¿Puedo tomar otro?	*pwedo tomar otro*
a loaf of bread	una barra de pan	*oona barra deh pan*

Buying **Things**

fruit & vegetables

apples	las manzanas	*las man**tha**nas*
apricots	los albaricoques	*los albaree**ko**kes*
artichokes	las alcachofas	*las alka**tcho**fas*
asparagus	los espárragos	*los es**parr**agos*
aubergines	las berenjenas	*las beren***che**nas*
avocado	el aguacate	*el agwa**ka**teh*
bananas	los plátanos	*los **pla**tanos*
beetroot	la remolacha	*la remol**atch**a*
cauliflower	la coliflor	*la kolee**flor***
celery	el apio	*el **a**peeo*
chard	las acelgas	*las a**thel**gas*
cherries	las cerezas	*las the**re**thas*
courgettes	los calabacines	*los kalaba**theen**es*
cucumber	el pepino	*el pe**pee**no*
figs	los higos	*los **ee**gos*
(black/green) grapes	las uvas (negras/verdes)	*las **oo**bas (**ne**gras/**ber**des)*
leeks	los puerros	*los **pwe**rros*
lemons	los limones	*los lee**mo**nes*
lettuce	la lechuga	*la let**choo**ga*
melon	el melón	*el me**lon***
mushrooms	los champiñones	*los champee**nyo**nes*
onions	las cebollas	*las the**bo**yas*
oranges	las naranjas	*las naran*chas*
peas	los guisantes	*los gee**san**tes*
peaches	los melocotones	*los meloko**to**nes*
pears	las peras	*las **pe**ras*
peppers	los pimientos	*los pee**meeyen**tos*
pineapple	la piña	*la **pee**nya*
plums	las ciruelas	*las theer**we**las*
potatoes	las patatas	*las pa**ta**tas*
raspberries	las frambuesas	*las fram**bwes**as*
strawberries	las fresas	*las **fre**sas*
tomatoes	los tomates	*los to**ma**tes*
watermelon	la sandía	*la san**dee**a*

check out 1

You're buying fruit at the market.

○ ¿Qué desea?
keh desea

- ¿Tiene melocotones?
teeyenay melokotones

○ No, no hay.
no no aee

- ¿A cuánto están los albaricoques?
a kwanto estan los albareekokes

○ A dos euros el kilo.
a dos eooros el keelo

- Déme dos kilos de albaricoques, y una sandía.
deme dos keelos deh albareekokes ee oona sandeea

○ Muy bien. ¿Algo más?
muiy beeyen. algo mas

- No, gracias. ¿Cuánto es?
no gratheeas. kwanto es

○ Son cinco euros treinta en total.
son theenko eooros traynta en total

Q What don't they have?
How much does it come to in total?

Buying **Things**

shopping for clothes

you may say ...

I'd like ...	Quisiera ...	kee**seeye**ra
a skirt.	una falda.	**oo**na falda
a tie.	una corbata.	**oo**na kor**ba**ta
some shoes.	zapatos.	tha**pa**tos
I'm just looking, thanks.	Gracias, sólo miraba.	gra**thee**as **s**olo mee**ra**ba
Do you have the same in ...	¿Tiene lo mismo en ...	teeye**nch** lo **mee**smo en
green?	verde?	**ber**deh
wool?	lana?	**la**na
cotton?	algodón?	algod**on**
silk?	seda?	**se**da
leather?	cuero?	**kwe**ro
I'm a size 40.	Soy la talla cuarenta.	soy la **ta**ya kwa**ren**ta
Can I ...	¿Puedo ...	**pwe**do
try it on?	probármelo/la?	pro**bar**melo/la
try them on?	probármelos/las?	pro**bar**melos/las
It's a bit big/small.	Es un poco grande/pequeño/a.	es oon **po**ko **gran**deh/pe**ken**yo/a
They're a bit big/small.	Son un poco grandes/pequeños/as.	son oon **po**ko **gran**des/pe**ken**yos/as
Have you anything ...	¿Tiene algo más ...	teeye**neh al**go mas
bigger?	grande?	**gran**deh
smaller?	pequeño/a?	pe**ken**yo/a
cheaper?	barato/a?	ba**ra**to/a
How much is it/are they?	¿Cuánto es/son?	**kwan**to es/son
I like it/them.	Me gusta/gustan.	meh **goos**ta/**goos**tan
I'll take it.	Me lo/la llevo.	meh lo/la **ye**bo
I'll take them.	Me los/las llevo.	meh los/las **ye**bo
I'll think about it.	Lo voy a pensar.	lo boy a pen**sar**
Do you take credit cards?	¿Aceptan tarjetas de crédito?	a**thep**tan tar*chetas deh **kre**deeto

you may hear ...

¿Qué talla/número?	*keh taya/noomero*	What size (clothes/shoes)?
Claro, por aquí.	*klaro por akee*	Of course, this way.
¿Le gusta/gustan?	*leh goosta/goostan*	Do you like it/them?
Le queda bien.	*leh keda beeyen*	It suits you.

clothes & accessories

belt	un cinturón	*oon theentooron*
boots	unas botas	*oonas botas*
coat	un abrigo	*oon abreego*
dress	un vestido	*oon besteedo*
hat	un sombrero	*oon sombrero*
jacket	una chaqueta	*oona chaketa*
jeans	unos vaqueros	*oonos bakeros*
knickers	una braga	*oona braga*
scarf	una bufanda	*oona boofanda*
shirt	una camisa	*oona kameesa*
socks	unos calcetines	*oonos kaltheteenes*
sweater	un suéter/jersey	*oon sweter/*cherseh*
swimming costume	un bañador	*oon banyador*
tie	una corbata	*oona korbata*
tights	unas medias	*oonas medeeas*
trousers	un pantalón	*oon pantalon*
T-shirt	una camiseta	*oona kameeseta*
underpants	un calzoncillo	*oon kalthontheeyo*
watch	un reloj	*oon relo*ch*

Buying **Things**

check out 2

You're shopping for a pair of trousers.

○ Buenas tardes. Quisiera un pantalón.
bwenas tardes. keeseeyera oon pantalon

- ¿De lana?
deh lana

○ No, de algodón. Talla cincuenta.
no deh algodon. taya theenkwenta

- ¿Le gusta éste?
leh goosta esteh

○ Sí. ¿Puedo probármelo?
see. pwedo probarmelo

- Claro, por aquí ... Le queda muy bien.
klaro por akee ... leh keda mooee beeyen

○ Vale, me lo llevo.
bale meh lo yebo

Q You want cotton trousers: true or false?
What size are you?

you may say ...

Where is the ... department?	¿Dónde está la sección de ...	*dondeh esta la sektheeon deh*
music	música?	*mooseeka*
food	alimentación?	*aleementatheeon*
ladies'/men's fashion	moda de señoras/ caballeros?	*moda deh senyoras/ kabayeros*
What floor is it on?	¿En qué planta está?	*en keh planta esta*
Is there a lift?	¿Hay ascensor?	*aee asthensor*
Where are the checkouts?	¿Dónde están las cajas?	*dondch estan las ka*chas*

you may hear ...

Está en la planta ...	*esta en la **plan**ta*	It's on the ... floor.
baja.	***ba***cha*	ground
primera.	*pree**me**ra*	first
segunda.	*se**goon**da*	second
tercera.	*ter**the**ra*	third
cuarta.	***kwar**ta*	fourth
el sótano	*el **so**tano*	basement

at the kiosk

you may say ...

Do you have any English newspapers/ English magazines?	¿Tiene periódicos ingleses/ revistas inglesas?	*teeyeneh pereeodee-kos een**gle**ses/ re**bees**tas een**gle**sas*
I'd like some ...	Quiero ...	*kee**ye**ro*
cigarettes.	cigarrillos.	*theega**rree**yos*
tobacco.	tabaco.	*ta**ba**ko*
cigars.	puros.	***poo**ros*
matches.	cerillas.	*the**ree**yas*
Do you have ...	¿Tiene ...	*tee**ye**neh*
a phone card?	una tarjeta telefónica?	***oo**na tar***che**ta telefo**nee**ka*
a lighter?	un mechero?	*oon me**tche**ro*

you may hear ...

sólo tengo ...	*solo **ten**go*	I only have ...
no tengo ...	*no **ten**go*	I don't have ...

Buying **Things**

photography

you may say ...

Can you develop this film, please?	¿Me revela este carrete?	*meh re**be**la esteh ka**rre**teh*
Can you print from this memory card?	¿Puede imprimir desde esta tarjeta de memoria?	*pwedeh eempree**meer** desdeh esta tar*cheta deh me**mo**reea*
When will it be ready?	¿Cuándo estará listo?	*kwando esta**ra lees**to*
normal/large size	tamaño normal/ grande	*ta**ma**nyo nor**mal**/ **gran**deh*
colour/black and white film	una película en color/ blanco y negro	*oona pe**lee**koola en ko**lor**/en **blan**ko ee **ne**gro*
a disposable camera	una cámara desechable	*oona **ka**mara dese**tcha**bleh*
(rechargeable) battery	una pila (recargable)	*oona **pee**la (rekar**ga**bleh)*

you may hear ...

mañana por la mañana/tarde	*man**ya**na por la man**ya**na/**tar**deh*	tomorrow morning/ afternoon
en una hora/ veinticuatro horas	*en **oo**na **o**ra/ bayntee**kwat**ro **o**ras*	in one hour/ 24 hours
¿Mate o brillante?	*mateh o bree**yan**teh*	Matt or gloss?
¿De qué tamaño?	*deh keh ta**ma**nyo*	What size?

at the post office

you may say ...

How much is a stamp for Europe?	¿Cuánto vale un sello para Europa?	*kwanto **ba**leh oon **se**yo para eoo**ro**pa*
for a letter/postcard	para carta/postal	*para **kar**ta/postal*
Two stamps, please.	Déme dos sellos.	*demeh dos **se**yos*
I'd like to send this to Ireland.	Quiero mandar esto a Irlanda.	*kee**ye**ro mandar **es**to a eer**lan**da*

sound check

r is strongly rolled, both at the beginning of a word:
revista *rebeesta*   rojo *ro*cho*   reloj *relo*ch*
and before a consonant:
verde *berdeh*   corbata *korbata*

rr (double **r**) is also always strongly rolled:
carro *karro*   barra *barra*
ferretería *ferretereea*

but the single **r** is pronounced more lightly before a vowel,
more like the 'r' in 'rain':
caro *karo*   cereza *theretha*

try it out

in the mix
Rearrange the syllables in these words to make things
you can eat or drink.

1 mozu
2 tanoplá
3 mónja
4 tóncomelo
5 chofaalca
6 soque
7 vohue
8 nadisar
9 janaran
10 zarece

match it up

Match each of these questions you might ask or hear when shopping with the best reply.

1 ¿En qué puedo servirle?
2 ¿Algo más?
3 ¿Qué número?
4 ¿Cuánto quiere?
5 ¿Cuánto es?
6 ¿A cuánto están las naranjas?

a El catorce.
b A cuatro euros el kilo.
c Déme quinientos gramos.
d ¿Tiene CD-ROM?
e Cinquenta euros.
f No, nada más, gracias.

as if you were there

You go into a grocer's shop one morning to buy things for a picnic. Follow the prompts to play your part.

Buenos días. ¿Qué desea?
(Ask for a hundred grammes of chorizo and two hundred grammes of cured ham)
Muy bien. ¿Algo más?
(Ask if they have any bread)
Sí. ¿Barra pequeña o grande?
(Say a large loaf)
¿Algo más?
(Say that's all, thanks, and ask how much)
Catorce euros ochenta.
(Hand over the money. Then say thank you and goodbye)

linkup

key phrases	¿**Tiene** albaricoques? — **Do you have** any apricots?
	Me gusta el vino tinto. — **I like** red wine.
	¿**Dónde está** la sección de música? — **Where's** the music department?
	Déme dos kilos. — **I'll have** two kilos.
	¿**Cuánto es** esta falda? — **How much is** this skirt?
	¿Tiene algo **más barato**? — Do you have anything **cheaper**?

asking about availability

There are two ways of asking this:

¿Tiene melocotones? Do you have any peaches?
¿Hay melocotones? Are there any peaches?

And the replies you are likely to hear are:

Sí, tengo melocotones. Yes, I've got (some) peaches.
No, no tengo melocotones. No, I don't have any peaches.
Sí, hay melocotones. Yes, we have (some) peaches.
No, no hay melocotones. No, we don't have any peaches.

Notice that in Spanish you don't need an extra word for 'some' or 'any'.

Note also that the useful word hay means both 'is there?/are there?' and 'there is/there are'.

comparing things

If you want something bigger, smaller, or cheaper use más:

¿Tiene una falda más pequeña? Do you have a smaller skirt?
Quiero algo más barato. I'd like something cheaper.

more than one

To talk about more than one of something is very easy in Spanish. You just add **-s** to a noun or adjective that ends in **-o**, **-a** or **-e**:

dos pimientos rojos two red peppers
un kilo de manzanas rojas a kilo of red apples

And you add **-es** to nouns and adjectives that end in a consonant (such as **-l**, **-n**, or **-r**):

cuatro melocotones blancos four white peaches
medio kilo de tomates grandes half a kilo of big tomatoes

Café **Life**

Spain has the most bars, cafés and restaurants per head of population in Europe, so you are sure to find something to suit your taste. It's not the custom in Spain to drink without eating, so all bars also offer a range of hot and cold **tapas** (snacks) and **raciones** (bigger helpings of the same). These are the snacks worth going to Spain for. Tapas can be almost anything – look for local specialities. Some of the more common ones are listed in this unit.

where to go

Cafés Busy from 7am until 9am with people breakfasting on strong coffee and **un bollo** (roll) or **una pasta** (pastry) and again between 6 and 8pm, when people stop for the **merienda**, an afternoon snack. Cafés are also good for sandwiches and tapas, and some offer more substantial midday meals. Look out for good value **platos combinados** (set dishes) or the **menú del día** (set menu), usually three courses and includes bread and a drink.

Bocadillerías These serve **bocadillos** (long sandwiches), **montados** (a half-sized version) and **sandwiches**, (toasted sandwich with cheese and ham), with chips and a drink.

Tascas Small and often very old bars full of character, serving tapas and raciones. They are usually tucked away in the narrow streets of the older parts of town.

Bodegas These are old, traditional bars selling wine, sherry and beer to drink in or take away. They usually have a wide selection of tapas and raciones on offer.

Cervecerías, tabernas and mesones Usually larger and with a greater if more expensive array of dishes. Many specialise in food from different regions of Spain.

Chiringuitos Small open-air bars, often on the beach, serving drinks and the occasional snack.

Heladerías Ice cream parlours.

speciality drinks

Wines Quality **Denominación de Origen** wines include Rioja and the young, light La Mancha and Valdepeñas; the pale dry Rueda or Ribera del Duero; and Albariño, a dry Galician white. Penedés are light wines while Priorato is a dark, heavy red with a velvety flavour. Campo de Borja and Somontano are heavy reds from Aragón; Navarra is excellent for reds, whites and rosés, while young Jumilla wines from Murcia, strong Alicante reds and rosés, and Valencia dry whites are also recommended.

Cava A delicious, inexpensive Spanish sparkling wine from Cataluña.

Jerez (sherry) Try the dry, light Fino; the amber medium Amontillado; the dark golden Oloroso and the sweet Moscatel.

Pacharán A raisin-based liqueur from Navarra.

Anís A strong dry or sweet alcoholic drink made from aniseed.

Orujo A strong Galician drink distilled from the grapes left over from wine-making. Try it in **la queimada**, made by burning the orujo in an earthenware pot with lemon, sugar and coffee beans.

Sangría A potent punch made with red wine, fruit juice and spirits.

Tinto de verano A refreshing mix of red wine and **gaseosa** (lemonade) with a dash of lemon juice.

Limón granizado A zesty summer drink made with fresh lemon, sugar and ground ice.

Horchata An unusual milky drink made from tiger nuts.

phrasemaker

asking what they have
you may say ...

Do you have ...	¿Tienen ...	*teeye*nen
ice creams?	helados?	e*la*dos
sandwiches?	bocadillos?	boka*dee*yos
Do you have any tapas?	¿Hay tapas?	aee *ta*pas
What ... do you have?	¿Qué ... tienen?	keh ... *teeye*nen
drinks	bebidas	be*bee*das
cold drinks	refrescos	re*fres*kos
sandwiches	bocadillos	boka*dee*yos
ice creams	helados	e*la*dos
flavours	sabores	sa*bores*
What do you have?	¿Qué tienen?	keh *teeye*nen

ordering
you may say ...

I'll have ...	Póngame ...	*pon*gameh
a portion of	una ración de	*oo*na ra*theeon* deh
omelette.	tortilla.	tor*tee*ya
a fizzy orange.	una naranjada.	*oo*na naran*cha*da
We'll have a portion of ham and some mushrooms.	Pónganos una ración de jamón y unos champiñones.	*pon*ganos *oo*na ra*theeon* deh *cha*mon ee oo*nos champee*nyon*es
A vanilla ice cream, please.	Un helado de vainilla, por favor.	oon e*la*do deh baee*neey*a por fa*bor*
A glass of white wine for me.	Para mí, un vaso de vino blanco.	*pa*ra mee, oon *ba*so deh *bee*no *blan*ko
This one.	Este.	*es*teh
That one.	Aquél.	a*kel*
How much is it?	¿Cuánto es?	*kwan*to es

Café **Life**

¿Qué desea(n)?	*keh desea(n)*	What would you like?
¿Quiere alguna tapa?	*keeyere algoona tapa*	Would you like any tapas?
Lo siento, no hay ...	*lo seeyento no aee*	Sorry, we don't have any ...
En seguida.	*en segeeda*	Right away.
Tenga./Aquí tiene.	*tenga/akee teeyene*	Here you are.
Tenemos helados de ...	*tenemos elados deh*	We have ... ice creams.
chocolate.	*chokolateh*	chocolate
fresa.	*fresa*	strawberry

soft drinks

cold chocolate	un chocolate frío	*oon chokolateh freeo*
fizzy lemon	una limonada	*oona leemonada*
fizzy orange	una naranjada	*oona naran*chada*
glass of milk	un vaso de leche	*oon baso deh letcheh*
milkshake	un batido	*oon bateedo*
iced coffee	un café con hielo	*oon kafeh kon eeyelo*
iced lemon drink	un granizado de limón	*oon graneethado deh leemon*
Iced melon drink	un granizado de melón	*oon graneethado deh melon*
lemonade	una gaseosa	*oona gasayosa*
... juice	un zumo de ...	*oon thoomo deh*
pineapple	piña	*peenya*
grapefruit	pomelo	*pomelo*
grape juice	un mosto	*oon mosto*
(sparkling/still) mineral water	un agua mineral (con gas/sin gas)	*oon agwa meeneral (kon gas/seen gas)*
tap water	agua del grifo	*agwa del greefo*
tea	un té	*oon teh*
tonic water	una tónica	*oona toneeka*
alcohol-free	sin alcohol	*seen alko'ol*
sparkling (wine)	(vino) espumoso	*(beeno) espoomoso*

alcoholic drinks

alcoholic drinks	bebidas alcohólicas	bebeedas alko'oleekas
anis(ette)	un anís	oon anees
aperitif	un aperitivo	oon apereeteebo
beer (bottled)	una cerveza	oona therbetha
bottle of Spanish sparkling wine	una botella de cava	oona boteya deh kaba
brandy	un coñac	oon konyak
liqueur coffee	un carajillo	oon kara*cheeyo
cider	una sidra	oona seedra
cuba libre (coke and white rum)	un cubalibre	oon koobaleebreh
dry sherry	un fino	oon feeno
glass of brandy	una copa de coñac	oona kopa deh konyak
brandy and aniseed liqueur	un sol y sombra	oon sol ee sombra
glass of draught beer	una caña	oona kanya
gin	una ginebra	oona *cheenebra
gin and tonic	un gintonic	oon geentoneek
a carafe of red/rosé wine	una garrafa de vino tinto/rosado	oona garrafa deh beeno teento/rosado

76

a glass of ... white wine	un vaso de vino blanco ...	*oon **ba**so deh **bee**no **blan**ko*
dry	seco	*se**ko**
sweet	dulce	***doo**ltheh*
semi-sweet	semi-seco	*se**mees**eko*
house	de la casa	*deh la **ka**sa*
local	del país	*del pa**ees***
table	de mesa	*deh **me**sa*
port	un oporto	*oon o**por**to*
rum	un ron	*oon ron*
sangría	una sangría	***oo**na san**gree**a*
shandy	una clara	***oo**na **kla**ra*
sherry	un jerez	*oon *che**reth**
vermouth	un vermú	*oon ber**moo***
vodka	un vodka	*oon **bod**ka*
whisky	un whisky	*oon **vees**kee*

check out 1

You're at a pavement café, ordering drinks.

○ Buenas tardes. ¿Qué desean?
 bwenas tardes. keh desean

- Buenas tardes. ¿Qué refrescos tienen?
 bwenas tardes. keh refreskos teeyenen

○ Tenemos zumo de piña y de naranja, granizado de limón y horchata.
 tenemos thoomo deh peenya ee deh naran*cha graneethado deh leemon ee ortchata

- Pónganos un granizado de limón y una cerveza.
 ***Pon**ganos oon graneethado deh leemon ee **oo**na therbetha*

○ Muy bien.
 mooee beeyen

Q Which three fruit drinks were you offered?

hot drinks

... coffee	un café ...	oon ka*feh*
black	solo	*so*lo
slightly white	cortado	kor*ta*do
creamy	con leche	kon *le*tcheh
decaffeinated	descafeinado	deskafehee*na*do
a cup of tea with milk/lemon	una taza de té con leche/limón	*oo*na *ta*tha deh teh kon *le*tcheh/lee*mon*
camomile tea	una manzanilla	*oo*na mantha*nee*ya
herbal tea	una infusión	*oo*na eenfoo*seeon*
hot chocolate	un chocolate caliente	oon choko*la*teh kalee*yen*teh
hot drinks	bebidas calientes	be*bee*das kalee*yen*tes
Irish coffee	un café irlandés	oon ka*feh* eerlan*des*
mint tea	un té de menta	oon teh deh *men*ta

check out 2

You stop for coffee while out shopping.

○ Buenas tardes, ¿qué desean?
  *bwe*nas *tar*des keh de*sean*

- Cuatro cafés.
  *kwa*tro ka*fes*

○ ¿Solos?
  *so*los

- No, uno solo y tres cortados.
  no *oo*no *so*lo ee tres kor*ta*dos

○ ¿Coñac?
  kon*yak*

- Sí, cuatro.
  see *kwa*tro

○ Muy bien.
  mooee bee*yen*

Q What do you all have as well as coffee?

78

Café **Life**

tapas

aceitunas	*athaytoonas*	olives
anchoas	*antchoas*	anchovies (salted)
atún	*atoon*	tuna
boquerones	*bokerones*	anchovies (fresh)
calamares a la romana	*kalamares a la romana*	fried squid
calamares en su tinta	*kalamares en soo teenta*	squid in its ink
caracoles de tierra/mar	*karakoles deh teeyerra/mar*	snails/whelks
champiñones	*champeenyones*	mushrooms
chorizo ibérico	*choreetho eebereeko*	spicy pork sausage made with paprika
empanadilla de ... carne pescado	*empanadeeya deh karneh peskado*	small ... pasty meat fish
ensaladilla rusa	*ensaladeeya roosa*	Russian salad
gambas a la plancha	*gambas a la plancha*	grilled prawns
jamón serrano	**chamon serrano*	cured ham
lomo de cerdo	*lomo deh therdo*	pork loin (pieces)
mejillones	*me*cheeyones*	mussels
patatas fritas	*patatas freetas*	crisps, chips
patatas all-oli	*patatas alee'olee*	garlic potatoes
patatas bravas	*patatas brabas*	fried potatoes in a spicy sauce
pincho moruno	*peentcho moroono*	marinated pork kebabs
pulpo	*poolpo*	octopus
queso manchego	*keso mantchego*	hard cheese from La Mancha
sardinas	*sardeenas*	sardines
sepia	*sepeea*	cuttlefish
tortilla española	*torteeya espanyola*	Spanish omelette

Bocadillos

Jamón Serrano 3€

Jamón York 2'5€

Jamón y Queso 3€

check out 3

You want to sample some tapas at a bodega.

- ○ Buenas tardes. ¿Qué tapas tienen?
  bwenas tardes. keh tapas teeyenen

- – Pues, hay calamares, gambas, tortilla española, queso, ensaladilla rusa ...
  pwes aee kalamares gambas torteeya espanyola keso ensaladeeya roosa

- ○ Pónganos una ración de gambas y una de tortilla y ... ¿hay patatas fritas?
  ponganos oona ratheeon deh gambas ee oona torteeya ee ... aee patatas freetas

- – ¡Claro! ¿Dos raciones?
  klaro. dos ratheeones

- ○ Sí, gracias y un fino y un vino tinto.
  see gratheeas ee oon feeno ee oon beeno teento

Q Which seafood tapas were you offered?

80

sound check

ch in Spanish is pronounced like the 'tch' in 'notch', wherever it occurs in a word.

chocolate   *choko**la**teh*   anchoas   *ant**cho**as*

Practise with these words:

horchata   *or**tcha**ta*   churros   ***choo**rros*

leche   *le**tch**eh*   champiñones   *champee**nyon**es*

try it out

allergies

Look at this tapas menu, and pick out those that would be suitable for a friend who is allergic to eggs and dairy produce and who doesn't like fish or seafood.

Gambas a la plancha	Chorizo	Anchoas
Boquerones	Aceitunas	Tortilla española
Empanadillas de carne	Mejillones	Queso manchego

as if you were there

You're sitting outside a café in the Plaza Mayor of Trujillo. Follow the prompts to play your part.

Buenas tardes, ¿qué desean?

(Greet him, and order a beer, a vermouth and a white wine)

Muy bien. ¿Quieren alguna tapa?

(Ask what they have)

Pues, tenemos chorizo, jamón serrano, tortilla, boquerones, patatas ali-oli, lomo de cerdo.

(Ask for a portion of ham, anchovies, chorizo and omelette)

Muy bien ...

(Ask how much it is)

Son trece euros con setenta y cinco.

linkup

key phrases		
¿**Tiene** bocadillos?	**Do you have** any sandwiches?
¿**Hay** tapas?	**Are there** any tapas?
Póngame una ración de tortilla.	**I'll have** a portion of omelette.
¿**Qué** refrescos **tiene**?	**What** cold drinks **do you have**?
Para mí una cerveza.	A beer **for me**.

requesting things

The easiest way is simply to say what you want:
Dos cervezas (por favor). Two beers, please.
You can add 'please', even though it's less common than in English. You can also say:
Para mí, una cerveza. A beer for me.

Here are a few more ways of saying 'Please could I have/ Please would you bring me a portion of omelette?':
Póngame una ración de tortilla.
¿Me pone una ración de tortilla?
Déme una ración de tortilla.
¿Me da una ración de tortilla?
Tráigame una ración de tortilla.
¿Me trae una ración de tortilla?

And another, very polite phrase:
¿Me hace el favor de traerme un cuchillo? Please could I have a knife?

Eating **Out**

when to eat

Eating out is cheap in Spain, and large family groups with children are always welcome. Lunchtime is between 2 and 4pm, when bars and cafés are filled with workers who don't have time to go home for the traditional midday meal. From 7pm onwards it's aperitif time, and then dinner is around 9 or 10pm. It's worth remembering that restaurants have relatively strict opening hours, and it can be very difficult to find one that will serve you outside these times.

Service is not usually included on bills in bars and restaurants. Tipping is not essential, but a **propina** (tip) of 10% is normal practice, and for small bills, 'rounding up' is common.

where to eat

Restaurantes These are the best places to have a tranquil sit-down meal. Generally, restaurants are classified from two to five forks, but many have no formal classification, yet serve wonderful typically Spanish food at very reasonable prices. Don't be put off if you think prices seem cheap; you may have come across a gem. All but the most exclusive restaurants have a **menú del día** or **menú especial**, but you can also eat as little or as much as you like by choosing individual items from the menu, tapas style. The à la carte selections tend to offer special regional dishes, and some international dishes.

Marisquerías These serve a tempting array of dishes prepared with ingredients fresh from the sea, even in cities far from the coast, and quality is generally guaranteed, though meals can be expensive.

courses

The Spanish diet is generally very healthy, with fruit and vegetables figuring highly in every menu (though vegetables tend to be fried in olive oil and garlic). Meat, fish and seafood are served plain or with a local sauce.

Entrada/Primer plato
A selection of salads, vegetables, cold meats, hot or cold soups or fish. **Entremeses** (hors d'oeuvres) are varied and delicious.

Plato principal/Segundo plato
Meat, fish, seafood, tortilla or pasta and a small garnish.

Postre Often home-made puddings or cakes, ice cream, custard tart, rice pudding or a piece of fruit. Don't forget the **copita** with your coffee – a shot or small glass of liqueur, brandy or whisky.

vegetarians

Vegetarian options can be limited; even vegetable dishes are often made with meat stock or contain pieces of meat. Salads and omelettes, especially the **tortilla española** or **tortilla de patatas**, are good fall-backs.

regional specialities

These include the following:
Andalusia Gazpacho (chilled soup made with fresh tomatoes, cucumber and garlic); **pescado en adobo** (fish in spicy batter).

Valencia Paella (saffron rice dish with mixed seafood and meat); **arroz empedrado** (rice with tomatoes, cod and white beans).

Galicia Pulpo gallego (griddled octopus with special seasoning). Asturias: **queso de cabrales** (extremely strong blue cheese).

El País Vasco Bacalao a la vizcaína (cod with peppers and onions); **angulas** (baby eels).

Aragón Pollo al chilindrón (chicken with tomato and pepper).

Barcelona Fideos a la cazuela (soup with noodles, spare ribs, sausage and bacon).

Castilla-León Cochinillo (whole roast suckling pig).

La Mancha Pisto manchego (stew made from fresh tomatoes, peppers and egg).

Madrid Cocido madrileño (hearty soup of meat, pulses and vegetables).

Islas Baleares El tumbet (potato and aubergine cake in tomato sauce).

(For drinks see pp75-78.)

phrasemaker

finding somewhere to eat

you may say ...

Is there a good restaurant near here?	¿Hay un buen restaurante por aquí?	*aee oon bwen restowranteh por akee*
Can you recommend a traditional restaurant?	¿Puede recomendar un restaurante tradicional?	*pwedeh rekomendar oon restowranteh tradeetheeonal*
I'd like to book a table for ...	Quiero reservar una mesa para ...	*keeyero reserbar oona mesa para*
tomorrow night.	mañana por la noche.	*manyana por la notcheh*
tonight at 8pm.	esta tarde a las ocho.	*esta tardeh a las otcho*

arriving

you may say ...

A table for two/four.	Una mesa para dos/cuatro.	*oona mesa para dos/kwatro*
We have a reservation for three.	Tenemos una reserva para tres.	*tenemos oona reserba para tres*
Do you have a high chair?	¿Tienen trona?	*teeyenen trona*

you may hear ...

Por aquí.	*por akee*	This way.
Lo siento, esta noche estamos al completo.	*lo seeyento, esta notcheh estamos al kompleto*	Sorry, we're full tonight.
Tendrán que esperar.	*tendran keh esperar.*	You'll have to wait.
¿Quieren beber algo?	*keeyeren beber algo*	Would you like anything to drink?

NTRECOT DE TERNERA CON
PATATAS Y ENSALADA

inicho de Tortilla 1'50€
ación de Tortilla 3'00€
- - -

APA DE ENSALADA DE
PALITOS CANGREJO 3€
- - -

PH AMB OL
- Con Jamón Serra
- Con Queso Mahon
- Con Atún
- Con Jamón y Queso
Pan Mallorquín con aceit

ENSALADAS

Verde 2.50€
Mixta 4€
Atún 3.65€

check out 1

You arrive at a restaurant and ask for a table for two.

○ Buenas tardes. ¿Una mesa para dos?
bwenas tardes. oona mesa para dos

- Sí, por aquí. ¿Quieren beber algo?
see por akee. keeyeren beber algo

○ Sí, un fino y un vermú.
see oon feeno ee oon bermoo

Q The waiter asks what you want to eat: true or false?

asking about the menu

you may say …

The menu, please.	La carta, por favor.	*la karta por fabor*
Is there a set menu?	¿Hay menú del día?	*aee menoo del deea*
What's the set menu?	¿Cuál es el menú del día?	*kwal es el menoo del deea*
Do you have any … fish soup? fillet steak? crab?	¿Tienen … sopa de pescado? solomillo? cangrejo?	*teeyenen sopa deh peskado solomeeyo kangre*cho*
Can you recommend anything?	¿Puede recomendar algo?	*pwedeh rekomendar algo*

Eating **Out**

Do you have ...	¿Hay ...	*aee*
vegetarian dishes?	platos vegetarianos?	*platos be*chetareeanos*
a kids' menu?	un menú para niños?	*un menoo para neenyos*
What is/are ...?	¿Qué es/son ...?	*keh es/son*
What is/are ... like?	¿Cómo es/son ...?	*komo es/son*
What's the local speciality?	¿Cuál es el plato típico de aquí?	*kwal es el plato teepeeko deh akee*
I'm ...	Soy ...	*soy*
vegetarian.	vegetariano/a.	*be*chetareeano/a*
vegan.	vegano/a.	*begano/a*
I don't eat ...	No como	*no komo*
meat.	carne.	*karneh*
fish.	pescado.	*peskado*
seafood.	mariscos.	*mareeskos*
Does it contain ...	¿Tiene	*teeyeneh*
chilli?	guindilla?	*geendeeya*
nuts?	nueces?	*nooethes*
I'm allergic to nuts.	Soy alérgico/a a los frutos secos.	*soy aler*cheeko/a a los frootos sekos*

ordering
you may say ...

... for me.	Para mí, ...	*para mee*
Garlic soup	una sopa de ajo.	*oona sopa deh a*cho*
Baked sea bream	un besugo al horno.	*oon besoogo al orno*
A pork chop	una chuleta de cerdo.	*oona chooleta deh therdo*
Could we have half a bottle of red wine? (See drinks, p75)	Tráiganos media botella de vino tinto.	*traeeganos medeea boteya deh beeno teento*
rare	poco hecho	*poko etcho*
medium	al punto	*al poonto*
well done	muy hecho	*mooee etcho*

you may hear …

¿Qué desean?	*keh desean*	What would you like?
¿Qué van a tomar de …	*keh ban a tomar deh*	What would you like as a …
primero?	*preemero*	first course?
segundo?	*segoondo*	main course?
¿Van a tomar postre?	*ban a tomar postreh*	Are you going to have any dessert?
¿Qué van a beber?/¿Y para beber?	*keh ban a beber/ ee para beber*	What would you like to drink?
El menú del día es …	*el menoo del deea es*	Today's set menu is …
Hoy tenemos …	*oy tenemos*	Today we have …
Lo siento, no hay …	*lo seeyento no aee*	Sorry, we don't have any …
¿Cómo lo quieren?	*komo lo keeyeren*	How would you like it?
Es …	*es*	It's …
un pescado blanco.	*oon peskado blanko*	a white fish.
una especie de tarta.	*oona espetheeyeh deh tarta*	a sort of tart.

check out 2

You have some questions about the menu.

○ ¿Qué van a tomar?
keh ban a tomar

- ¿Qué es ensalada 'El Chato'?
keh es ensalada el chato

○ Es la ensalada de la casa. Es muy buena.
es la ensalada deh la kasa. es mooee bwena

- Bueno, de primero una sopa de pescado y una ensalada.
bweno deh preemero oona sopa deh peskado ee oona ensalada

○ ¿Y de segundo?
ee deh segoondo

- Un besugo al horno y un solomillo.
oon besoogo al orno ee oon solomeeyo

○ Lo siento, hoy no hay besugo.
lo seeyento oy no aee besoogo

- Entonces una chuleta de cerdo.
entonthes oona chooleta deh therdo

○ ¿Y para beber?
ee para beber

- Una botella de vino blanco y una botella de agua mineral con gas.
oona boteya deh beeno blanko ee oona boteya deh agwa meeneral kon gas

(entonces = then)

 Q
What do you have for starters?
Which item is off the menu today?

during the meal

you may say ...

Excuse me!	¡Oiga!	*oyga*
More bread/wine, please.	Más pan/vino, por favor.	*más pan/**bee**no por fa**bor***
They're very good.	Están muy buenos/buenas.*	*están mooee **bwe**nos/**bwe**nas*
It's ...	Está ...	*está*
very good.	muy bueno/bueno.*	*mooee **bwe**no/a*
delicious.	muy rico/rica.*	*mooee **ree**ko/a*
cold.	frío/fría.*	*free*o/a
very hot. (spicy)	muy picante.	*mooee pee**kan**te*
raw.	crudo/cruda.*	***kroo**do/a*

you may hear ...

¿Todo bien?	*todo bee**yen***	Everything okay?
¿Qué tal la merluza?	*keh tal la mer**loo**tha*	How's the hake?
¿Qué tal las croquetas?	*keh tal las kro**ke**tas*	How are the croquettes?
¿Algo más?	***al**go mas*	Anything else?

(*For more on which ending to use, see the Language Builder, p135.)

Eating **Out**

on your table

ashtray	el cenicero	*el theneethero*
fork	el tenedor	*el tenedor*
knife	el cuchillo	*el kootcheeyo*
napkin	la servilleta	*la serbeeyeta*
oil	el aceite	*el athayeeteh*
plate	el plato	*el plato*
salt/pepper	la sal/la pimienta	*la sal/la peemeeyenta*
saucer	el platillo	*el plateeyo*
spoon	la cuchara	*la kootchara*
tablecloth	el mantel	*el mantel*
teaspoon	la cucharilla	*la kootchareeya*
vinegar	el vinagre	*el beenagreh*

paying the bill

you may say ...

The bill, please.	La cuenta, por favor.	*la kwenta por fabor*
Is service included?	¿Está incluido el servicio?	*esta eenklweedo el serbeetheeo*
Do you take credit cards?	¿Aceptan tarjetas de crédito?	*atheptan tar*chetas deh kredeeto*
There's a mistake, I think.	Hay un error, creo.	*aee oon error krayo*
We didn't have this.	No tomamos esto.	*no tomamos esto*

you may hear ...

El servicio ...	*el serbeetheeo*	Service ...
no está incluido.	*no esta eenklweedo*	is not included.
es extra.	*es estra*	is extra.

check out 3

It's time to pay your bill.

- ○ ¡Camarera! La cuenta, por favor.
  kamarera la kwenta por fabor

- – En seguida … Aquí tiene.
  en segeeda … akee teeyeneh

- ○ ¿Aceptan tarjetas de crédito?
  atheptan tar*chetas deh kredeeto

- – Sí, Visa y Mastercard.
  see beesa ee masterkard

- ○ Muy bien.
  mooee beeyen

Q Do they accept credit cards?

sound check

j in Spanish is pronounced like the 'ch' in the Scottish pronunciation of 'loch', written in this book as **ch*:

cangrejo *kangre*cho*   ajo *a*cho*

Practise with these words:

mejillones *me*cheeyones*	jerez **chereth*
lentejas *lente*chas*	jabalí **chabalee*

92

Eating **Out**

try it out

match it up

Can you match the English words with their Spanish equivalents?

1	red wine	**a**	la ensalada
2	hake	**b**	las nueces
3	salad	**c**	la cuchara
4	fish	**d**	el vino tinto
5	spoon	**e**	el pescado
6	nuts	**f**	la merluza

as if you were there

You go to a fish restaurant in Santander, on the north coast, for dinner. Follow the prompts to play your part.

(Greet the waiter and say you'd like a table for two)
Muy bien … ¿Quieren beber algo?
(Ask for a glass of red wine and a sherry)
The waiter comes back after you've looked at the menu.
¿Qué van a tomar?
(Ask what the 'langostas a la santanderina' are like)
Son muy buenas, a la plancha con un poco de ajo, pero poco.
(Sounds nice! Order two of them, and a garlic soup and a salad)
The waiter comes up again.
¿Qué tal la langosta?
(Tell him it's great)
¿Van a tomar postre?
(Say no thank you, and ask for the bill)

linkup

key phrases		
¿Qué es besugo al horno?	**What is** besugo al horno?
¿Cómo son los fideos a la cazuela?	**What are** fideos a la cazuela like?
Voy a tomar la sopa.	**I'm going to have** the soup.
Para mí el gazpacho.	The gazpacho **for me**.
Tráigame más pan, por favor.	**Could you bring me** more bread, please?

talking to you

In Spanish, when talking to one person there are two different words for 'you'. The formal/polite word for 'you' is usted; the more friendly word is tú. You use usted when talking to someone you don't know very well, and tú when talking to someone you know well. The word itself may often be missed out, but the ending you put on the verb changes depending on which one you use.

A waiter would say to you:

¿Qué quier**e** tomar? What would you like? (formal)

But to a friend, or someone you know fairly well you'd say:

¿Qué quier**es** tomar? What would you like? (informal)

With the usted form, the ending of the verb is usually an **a** or an **e**:

¿Dónde viv**e**? Where do you live?
¿Dónde trabaj**a**? Where do you work?

If you choose the tú form, there's an **s** at the end:

¿Dónde vive**s**?, ¿Dónde trabaja**s**?
The verb ending also changes if you are talking to more than one person:

¿Dónde viven (ustedes)?   Where do you live? (formal)
¿Dónde trabajáis (vosotros)?   Where do you work? (informal)

But fortunately this is much less common than talking to just one person!

For more on 'you', see the Language Builder, p133.······▷

saying what you are going to do

To say what you're going to do use voy a (I'm going to) followed by an infinitive:

Voy a tomar el pescado.   I'll have the fish.
Vamos a tomar una copa.   We're going to have a drink.
¿Qué van a tomar?   What are you going to have?

menus and courses

la carta menu
el menú del día fixed-price menu
el plato del día dish of the day
los platos combinados set dishes
las entradas starters
el primer plato first course
el segundo plato main course
los postres desserts
pan y cubierto bread and cover charge
pan y vino incluidos bread and wine included
servicio (no) incluido service (not) included

main ways of cooking

adobo (al) pickled/marinated
ahumado/a smoked
asado/a roast
brasa (a la) barbecued
catalán (a la) Catalan-style, with onion, tomato and herbs
cazuela (a la) casseroled
cocido/a boiled/stewed
crudo/a raw
empanado/a breaded and fried
escabechado/a/
en escabeche pickled/soused/marinated
estofado/a stewed
frito/a fried
guisado/a stewed
gusto (a su) to your taste
hervido/a boiled
horno (al) baked
natural (al) fresh/raw
parrilla (a la) barbecued/grilled
picado/a minced

plancha (a la) grilled (on a griddle)
rebozado/a battered/breaded and fried
rehogado/a sautéed
relleno/a stuffed
romano (a la) deep fried in batter
salteado/a sautéed
vapor (al) steamed

main sauces

a la crema creamed/in cream sauce
ajillo (al) with garlic and oil
alioli/allioli garlic mayonnaise
chilindrón (al) with dried red peppers, tomato and ham
encebollado/a tomato with onions
gratinado/a with melted cheese
marinera (a la) in fish or seafood and tomato sauce
pil-pil (al) with chilli
romesca dried red peppers, almonds and garlic
verde green sauce, parsley, onion and garlic
vinagreta vinaigrette

the menu

aceitunas olives
aguacate avocado
ajo garlic
albóndigas meatballs
alcachofas artichokes
almejas clams
almendras almonds
alubias beans
  blancas butter beans
  pintas red kidney beans
anchoas anchovies

apio celery
arenque herring
arroz rice
  a la cubana rice with tomato sauce and fried egg
atún tuna
avellana hazelnut
aves poultry
bacalao cod
  a la vizcaína Basque-style with peppers, ham and chilli
berberechos cockles
berenjena aubergine
berza cabbage
besugo sea bream
bistec grilled steak
bonito tuna, tunny
boquerones anchovies
brocheta skewer/kebab
brócoli broccoli
buey/de buey ox
butifarra a type of white sausage from Cataluña
caballa mackerel
cabrito kid
cacahuetes peanuts
calabacín courgette
calabaza marrow/pumpkin
calamares squid
caldereta stew

caldo clear soup
  gallego vegetable, bean and pork soup
callos tripe
  a la madrileña Madrid-style tripe, in a spicy sausage and tomato sauce
camarones baby prawns, shrimps
cangrejo crab
caracoles snails
carne meat
castaña chestnut
caza game
cebolla onion
cerdo pork
champiñones mushrooms
chipirones baby squid
chorizo spicy sausage
chuleta de cerdo pork chop
cigalas crayfish
col cabbage
cuajada junket
embutidos cold meats
emperador type of swordfish
endivias chicory
ensalada salad
ensaladilla rusa Russian salad (diced potatoes and vegetables in mayonnaise)
entrecot steak

escalope escalope
  a la milanesa breaded veal
  with cheese
escarola endive
espárragos asparagus
espinacas spinach
faisán pheasant
fiambre mixed cold meat
fideos noodles
filete fillet
fritura de pescado mixed fried
fish
gallina hen
gambas prawns/shrimps
ganso goose
garbanzos chickpeas
guisantes peas
habas broad beans
habichuelas haricot beans
hierbas herbs
hígado liver
hinojo fennel
huevas fish eggs/roe eggs
huevos eggs
  cocidos/duros hard boiled
  escalfados poached
  revueltos scrambled
  a la flamenca Andalusian-
  style, baked with spicy
  sausage, tomato, peas,
  asparagus
jabalí wild boar
jamón ham
  de york cooked ham
  serrano cured ham
judías beans
  blancas haricot beans
  verdes green/French beans
lacón type of cooked pork
langosta lobster
langostino king prawn
lechuga lettuce
lengua tongue
lenguado sole
lentejas lentils

aliñadas lentils with
  vinaigrette
liebre hare
lombarda red cabbage
lomo de cerdo loin of pork
longaniza type of spicy
sausage
lubina sea bass
macarrones gratinados
macaroni cheese
mahonesa mayonnaise
maíz sweetcorn
manos de cerdo pig's trotter
mantequilla butter
mariscada mixed shellfish
mariscos seafood
medallones medallions
mejillones mussels
membrillo quince jelly
menestra de verduras
vegetable soup/stew
merluza hake
  a la gallega hake with
  paprika and tomatoes
mixto/a mixed
morcilla black pudding
mostaza mustard
nabo turnip
nata cream
nueces walnuts
ostras oysters
paella rice dish
  valenciana with seafood
  catalana with meat and
  squid
pan bread
  con tomate
  bread rubbed with garlic and
  tomato
panaché de legumbres/
verduras mixed vegetables
panceta bacon
parrillada mixed grill
patatas potatoes
patatas fritas chips

pato duck
pavo turkey
pechuga de pollo chicken breast
pepinillo gherkin
pepino cucumber
perdiz partridge
perejil parsley
pescadilla whiting
pescado fish
pescaditos fried small fish
pez espada swordfish
picadillo minced meat/sausage
picatoste croutons
pimentón paprika
pimienta pepper
pinchos morunos small kebabs
piñones pine kernels
pisto sautéed vegetable mix
plato de fiambres mixed cold meats
pollo chicken
potaje thick vegetable soup
puerros leeks
pulpo octopus
puntas de espárragos asparagus tips
puré de patatas mashed potatoes
queso cheese
  de bola round, mild cheese (like Edam)
  de Burgos soft cream cheese
  de cabra goat's milk cheese
  de cabrales strong blue cheese
  de oveja sheep's milk cheese
  fresco curd cheese
  manchego hard cheese
quisquillas shrimps
rábano radish
rabo de buey oxtail

rape angler/monk fish
raya skate
remolacha beetroot
repollo cabbage
requesón curd/cream cheese
riñones kidneys
rodaballo turbot
salami salami
salchicha sausage
salchichón salami-type sausage
salmón salmon
salmonete red mullet
salpicón de mariscos shellfish with vinaigrette
salvia sage
samfaina mixture of onion, tomato, peppers, aubergine and courgette
sardinas sardines
sepia cuttlefish
sesos brains
setas wild mushrooms
sobrasada type of sausage (from Mallorca)
solomillo fillet steak
sopa soup
  castellana vegetable soup
  de ajo garlic soup
  de picadillo chicken, meat, noodle soup
  juliana mixed vegetable soup
ternera veal
tomate tomato
tortilla omelette
  a la paisana with mixed vegetables
  francesa plain
  española/de patata Spanish
tostadas toast
trucha trout
(carne de) vaca beef
variados/as assorted
venado venison

verduras vegetables
vieiras scallops
zanahorias carrots
zarzuela de (pescados y) mariscos spicy (fish and) seafood stew

desserts

arroz con leche rice pudding
chirimoya custard apple
chocolate chocolate
flan crème caramel
fruta fresh fruit (See p61 for fruit)
helado ice cream
  mantecado dairy ice cream
leche frita thick slices of custard fried in breadcrumbs
macedonia de frutas fruit salad
merengada milk and meringue sorbet

mazapán marzipan
mermelada (de naranja) jam/ marmalade
miel honey
natillas egg custard
pastel cake
repostería pastries
sopa de almendra almond-based pudding
sorbete sorbet
tarta cake/tart
  helada ice cream gateau
  de manzana apple tart
tocinillo de cielo/tocinitos rich crème caramel
torrijas sugar and cinnamon bread
turrón almond and honey christmas sweet
yemas meringue, brandy and sugar

Entertainment

finding out what's on

Local tourist offices provide a host of useful information, often in English. Look out also for English-language newspapers in tourist resorts. You could also try the listings pages of local and national newspapers such as *El País*, *El Mundo* and the *Guía del Ocio* in Madrid and Barcelona.

what to see

Football The Spanish are mad about football and, if you can't make a live game, it's worth watching an important match in a packed bar. Top live venues are Real Madrid's Bernabéu Stadium, Atlético Madrid's Vicente Calderón Stadium, Barcelona's Nou Camp and Seville's Sánchez Pizjuán Stadium. The season runs from September to June and games are normally on Sundays.

Bullfights Between March and October, **los toros** (bulls) are an important part of the Spanish calendar. The most famous bullrings are Las Ventas in Madrid and Seville's Maestranza. Bullfights traditionally start around 6pm.

Fairs and festivals The Spanish like a celebration, and local festivals are a great opportunity to sample local specialities and hear traditional music. Key dates are the religious celebrations during Easter week and on August 15th, as well as El Día de la Hispanidad on October 12th.

Flamenco This guitar, singing and dancing is best heard in its native Andalusia, but can be just as impressive if you go to a flamenco club or bar in a major city or resort. Salsa and other Latin American rhythms are very popular in Spain.

Folk music Always popular in Spain, this is now undergoing something of a resurgence. Galicia and Asturias are proud of their Celtic roots, and regional language folk groups can also be found in Euskadi (Basque Country), Cataluña, the Balearic Islands and Valencia.

Cinema Foreign films may be shown in the original language version, though many are dubbed into Spanish. Tickets are relatively cheap and you can may be able to take advantage of **el día de las parejas** (mid-week reductions): two tickets for the price of one.

sports

Winter sports Spain has six well-equipped winter sports resort areas, in the Catalan Pyrenees, the Aragón Pyrenees, the Cantabrian Mountains, the Iberian range near La Rioja, the Central Range near Madrid and the exceptional range of Sierra Nevada in Granada. The season lasts roughly from December to April.

Swimming The Mediterranean coasts are wonderful for safe swimming, especially between May and September. Few Spaniards take a dip out of these months, considering the water too cold. Open-air pools open from mid-May to mid-September.

Sailing There are about 250 mooring points for leisure craft around the coast, where you can rent boats or yachts with or without crew. Check local marinas or tourist offices for information.

Surfing This is big on the Cantabrian coast around Zarauz and Mundaka, where surf competitions are held, and at windy Tarifa on the south coast.

Walking There are over 1,226 square kilometres of spectacular National Parks which are ideal for walking. Try the waterfalls and glacial valleys of the Pyrenees. Check with the nearest tourist office for local routes. Go on a weekday, and you will probably meet no one else on your ramble.

Hunting Spain has a rich variety of fauna, so hunting is tightly controlled. The season starts in mid-October. Deer, chamois, wild boar and Spanish ibex as well as partridge, quail and duck are widely hunted, but check tourist offices or the **Comunidades Autónomas** (regional regulating bodies) for details.

Fishing Sea fishing off the Mediterranean, Cantabrian and Atlantic coasts offers fish from mullet to tuna. Salmon, trout, pike and sturgeon are among the dozens of species lurking in over 75,000 km of inland rivers. Hunting and fishing licences can be obtained from the **Agencia de Medio Ambiente** in each regional capital.

Horseriding Generally considered a pastime of the wealthy, but if you venture out into the villages you can often find small riding schools charging a very reasonable rate.

Golf There are more than 100 courses in Spain, mostly on the Mediterranean coast and the islands and around Madrid, and more are being built. Almost all clubs give temporary permits to foreign visitors looking for a game.

Tennis Most cities, towns and resorts have public courts.

children

Spain has a range of entertainment and activities for children. The best-known theme parks are Terra Mítica near Benidorm, Port Aventura in Tarragona, Isla Mágica in Seville, and the Warner Brothers park in Madrid. Zoos, aquariums and nature parks offer interactive entertainment for children, and the chance to observe a wide range of wildlife. Try Barcelona Zoo, Valencia's L'Oceanográfic aquarium and the Cuenca Alta del Manzanares in La Pedriza (natural environment), Madrid, Estepona, (birds and land animals) and Benalmádena, (marine animals).

phrasemaker

getting to know the place

you may say ...

Where is ...	¿Dónde ésta ...	*don*deh es*ta*
the Tourist Office?	la Oficina de Turismo?	la ofee*thee*na deh too*ree*smo
the beach?	la playa?	*la play*a
the cathedral?	la catedral?	la kate*dral*
the theatre?	el teatro?	el tea*tro*
Do you have ...	¿Tiene ...	*teeye*neh
a map of the town?	un plano/mapa de la ciudad?	oon *plan*o/*mapa* deh la thee*ooda*
an entertainment guide?	una guía de espectáculos?	*oo*na *gee*a deh espek*ta*koolos
Do you have any information in English?	¿Tiene información en inglés?	*teeye*neh eenforma*theeon* en een*gles*
Are there any ...	¿Hay ...	*aee*
cinemas?	cine?	*thee*neh
concerts?	conciertos?	konthee*yer*tos
parks?	parques?	*par*kes
nightclubs?	discotecas?	deesko*te*kas
What is there to see/ do here?	¿Qué se puede ver/ hacer aquí?	keh seh *pwe*deh ber/ a*ther* a*kee*
Is there a ... tour?	¿Hay una visita ...	*aee oo*na bee*see*ta
guided	con guía?	kon *gee*a
bus	en autobús?	en owto*boos*
Is there anything for children?	¿Hay algo para los niños?	*aee al*go *pa*ra los *nee*nyos
Can you recommend ...	¿Puede recomendar ...	*pwe*deh rekomen*dar*
a museum?	un museo?	oon moo*sayo*
an exhibition?	una exposición?	*oo*na esposee*theeon*
a bar?	un bar?	oon bar

Entertainment

I like ...	Me gusta ...	meh **goos**ta
classical/pop music.	la música clásica/el pop.	la **moo**seeka **klas**eeka/el pop
modern art.	el arte moderno.	el **ar**teh mo**der**no
football.	el fútbol.	el **foot**bol
I don't like ...	No me gustan ...	no meh **goos**tan
bullfights.	las corridas de toros.	las ko**rree**das deh **to**ros
fireworks.	los fuegos artificiales.	los **fwe**gos arteefeethee**a**les

you may hear ...

Hay una visita ...	aee **oo**na bee**see**ta	There is a tour ...
todos los días.	**to**dos los **dee**as	every day.
los fines de semana.	los **fee**nes deh se**ma**na	at weekends.
Está cerca/lejos.	es**ta ther**ka/**le***chos	It's near/far.
Hay muchos monumentos interesantes.	aee **moo**tchos monoo**men**tos intere**san**tes	There are lots of interesting sights.
Hay ...	aee	There is ...
el castillo/ el alcázar.	el kas**tee**yo/ el al**ka**thar	the castle.
el puente viejo.	el **pwen**teh bee**ye***cho	the old bridge.
el palacio.	el pa**la**theeo	the palace.
una exposición de ...	**oo**na esposee**theeon** deh	an ... exhibition
arte	**ar**teh	art
pintura	peen**too**ra	painting
cerámica	the**ra**meeka	ceramics
fotografía	fotogra**fee**a	photography
¿Le gusta ...	leh **goos**ta	Do you like ...
el flamenco?	el fla**men**ko	flamenco?
la música?	la **moo**seeka	music?
bailar?	baee**lar**	dancing?
el deporte?	el de**por**teh	sport?
¿Qué le gusta?	keh leh **goos**ta	What do you like?

check out 1

You ask about local attractions at the tourist office.

○ ¿Qué se puede ver en Salamanca?
keh seh pwedeh ber en salamanka

- Pues, hay muchos monumentos interesantes: la Catedral Nueva, la Catedral Vieja y el puente romano.
pwes aee mootchos monoomentos eenteresantes la katedral nweba la katedral beeye*cha ee el pwente romano

○ ¿Hay conciertos de música clásica?
aee kontheeyertos deh mooseeka klaseeka

- Sí, los fines de semana.
see los feenes deh semana

○ Gracias.
gratheeas

> **Q** What sights are recommended?
> You can hear classical music at weekends: true or false?

getting more information

you may say ...

Where is ...	¿Dónde está ...	*dondeh esta*
the swimming pool?	la piscina?	*la peestheena*
the art gallery?	la galería de arte?	*la galereea deh arteh*
the stadium?	el estadio?	*el estadeeo*
Where does the tour start?	¿Dónde empieza la visita?	*dondeh empeeyetha la beeseeta*

What time does (it) ... start/finish?	¿A qué hora empieza/termina ...	a keh ora empeeyetha/termeena
the opera	la opera?	la opera
the football match	el partido de fútbol?	el parteedo deh footbol
the show	el espectáculo?	el espektakoolo
the (music) festival	el festival (de música)?	el festeebal (deh mooseeka)
the festival	la fiesta?	la feeyesta
the film	la película?	la peleekoola
How much does it cost?	¿Cuánto cuesta/vale?	kwanto kwesta/baleh
What are the opening hours?	¿Qué horario tiene?	keh orareeo teeyeneh
Is it open ...	¿Abre ...	abreh
on Mondays?	los lunes?	los loones
at the weekend?	los fines de semana?	los feenes deh semana
Is there wheelchair access?	¿Hay acceso para minusválidos?	aee aktheso para meenoosbaleedos
How long does it last?	¿Cuánto tiempo dura?	kwanta teeyempo doora
Does it have subtitles in English?	¿Tiene subtítulos en inglés?	teeyeneh soobteetoolos en eengles
Is there an interval?	¿Hay un descanso?	aee oon deskanso
Are there any tickets for the concert?	¿Hay entradas para el concierto?	aee entradas para el kontheeyerto
Do you need tickets?	¿Se necesitan entradas?	seh netheseetan entradas
Where do you buy tickets?	¿Dónde se compran las entradas?	dondeh seh kompran las entradas

you may hear ...

No se necesitan entradas.	no seh netheseetan entradas.	You don't need tickets.
Es gratuita/o.	es gratweeta/o	It's free.
Lo siento, están agotadas.	lo seeyento estan agotadas	Sorry, it's sold out.

En la Plaza Mayor, a las diez.	*en la platha mayor a las deeyeth*	In the main square, at 10 o'clock.
Cierran ... los domingos. en invierno.	*theeyerran los domeengos en eenbeeyerno*	It is closed ... on Sundays. in the winter.
Empieza .../ Termina ... a las siete de la tarde. a las diez de la noche.	*empeeyetha/ termeena a las seeyeteh deh la tardeh a las deeyeth deh la notcheh*	It starts .../ It finishes ... at 7pm. at 10pm.
Dura dos/tres horas.	*doora dos/tres oras*	It is two/three hours long.
desde ... hasta ...	*desdeh ... asta*	from ... to ...
En la taquilla.	*en la takeeya*	At the ticket office.
Aquí, en el plano.	*akee en el plano*	Here, on the map.

check out 2

You want to check out the local nightlife.

○ ¿Dónde está la discoteca 'La Sevillana'?
dondeh esta la deeskoteka la sebeeyana

- Está en la calle de Serrano, aquí en el mapa.
esta en la kayeh deh serrano akee en el mapa

○ Y ¿a qué hora abre?
ee a keh ora abreh

- A las once, aproximadamente.
a las ontheh aproseemadamenteh

○ Y ¿se necesitan entradas?
ee seh netheseetan entradas

- No. La entrada es gratuita.
no. la entrada es gratweeta

Q 'La Sevillana' opens at about eight o'clock: true or false?
Do you need to buy tickets?

getting in

you may say ...

Are there any tickets for tonight/ tomorrow?	¿Hay entradas para esta noche/ mañana?	*aee entradas para esta notcheh/ manyana*
How much are they?	¿Cuánto valen?	***kwan**to **ba**len*
Is there a concession for ...	¿Hay descuentos para ...	*aee des**kwen**tos para*
children?	niños?	***nee**nyos*
students?	estudiantes?	*estoodee**an**tes*
pensioners?	pensionistas?	*penseeo**nees**tas*
people with disabilities?	minusválidos?	*meenoos**ba**leedos*
Two stalls/circle tickets, please.	Dos entradas de platea/anfiteatro.	*dos en**tra**das deh pla**te**a/anfeete**a**tro*
I'd like a programme.	Quiero un programa.	*kee**ye**ro oon pro**gra**ma*
Is this seat taken/free?	¿Está ocupado/libre este asiento?	*es**ta** okoo**pa**do/**lee**breh **es**teh a**see**yento*
Where is the cloakroom?	¿Dónde está el guardarropa?	***don**deh es**ta** el gwarda**rro**pa*

Está libre/ ocupado.	esta *lee*breh/ okoo*pa*do	It is available/ taken.
Hay asientos en el 'gallinero'.	aee a*see*yentos en el gayee*ne*ro	We have got seats in the 'gods'.
Está todo ocupado esta noche.	esta *to*do okoo*pa*do *es*ta *no*tcheh	We are full tonight.
Pueden sentarse donde quieran.	*pwe*den sen*tar*seh *don*deh kee*eye*ran	You can sit where you like.

sports

you may say ...

Where can you play ...	¿Dónde se puede jugar al ...	*don*deh seh *pwe*deh *choo*gar al
tennis?	tenis?	*te*nees
golf/18 holes?	golf/dieciocho hoyos?	golf/deeyetheeotcho *oy*os
Where can you go ...	¿Dónde se puede hacer ...	*don*deh seh *pwe*deh a*ther
surfing?	surfing?	*soor*feeng
walking?	senderismo?	sender*ees*mo
climbing?	alpinismo?	alpee*nees*mo
fishing?	pesca?	*pe*ska
waterskiing?	esquí acuático?	es*kee* akwa*teeko*
mountain biking?	ciclismo de montaña?	thee*klees*mo deh mon*tan*ya
Is it okay to swim here?	¿Puedo bañarme aquí?	*pwe*do ban*yar*meh a*kee*
Is it dangerous?	¿Es peligroso?	es pelee*gro*so
Can I hire waterskis?	¿Se pueden alquilar esquíes acuáticos?	seh *pwe*den alkee*lar* es*kees* ak*wa*teekos
Can I hire ...	¿Se puede alquilar ...	seh *pwe*deh alkee*lar*
a tennis racket?	una raqueta de tenis?	*oo*na ra*ke*ta deh *te*nees
a windsurf board?	una tabla de windsurf?	*oo*na *tab*la deh *ween*soorf
a sunshade?	una sombrilla?	*oo*na som*bree*ya
a sun lounger?	una tumbona?	*oo*na toom*bo*na

Entertainment

Can I use the hotel pool?	¿Puedo utilizar la piscina del hotel?	*pwedo ooteeleethar la peestheena del otel*
I'd like to take ... lessons.	Quisiera tomar clases de ...	*keeseeyera tomar klases deh*
sailing	vela.	*bela*
skiing	esquí.	*eskee*
windsurfing	windsurf.	*weensoorf*
Can children do it too?	¿Los niños también lo pueden hacer?	*los neenyos tambeeyen lo pweden ather*
Where are ...	¿Dónde están	*dondeh estan*
the changing rooms?	los vestuarios?	*los bestooareeos*
the showers?	las duchas?	*las dootchas*

you may hear ...

Cuesta veinte euros por hora/día.	*kwesta baynteh eooros por ora/deea*	It's €20 per hour/day.
¿Quiere tomar alguna clase?	*keeyereh tomar algoona klaseh*	Would you like to take any lessons?
Cerca de la playa hay ...	*therka deh la playa aee*	There is ... near the beach.
una cancha de tennis.	*oona kantcha deh tenees*	a tennis court
un campo de golf.	*oon kampo deh golf*	a golf course

sports equipment

balls	las pelotas	*las pelotas*
boat	una barca	***oo**na **bar**ka*
golf clubs	los palos de golf	*los **pa**los deh golf*
ice skates	los patines de hielo	*los pa**tee**nes deh **ee**yelo*
ski boots	las botas de esquí	*las **bo**tas deh es**kee***
skis	los esquíes	*los es**kees***
snowboard	la plancha de nieve	*la **plan**tcha deh **nee**yebeh*

check out 3

At the beach you decide to try windsurfing.

○ ¿Se puede hacer wind-surf aquí?
*seh **pwe**deh a**ther ween**soorf a**kee***

- Sí. ¿Quiere tomar alguna clase?
*see. kee**ye**ray to**mar** al**goo**na **kla**seh*

○ ¿Cuánto cuesta?
***kwan**to **kwes**ta*

- Veinticuatro euros por hora.
*bayntee**kwa**tro **e**ooros por **o**ra*

○ Vale.
***ba**leh*

Q How much is a windsurf lesson?

sound check

When a **c** in Spanish is not followed by an **e** or an **i**, it is pronounced like the 'k' in 'kit':

concierto   *kontheeyerto*   cerámica   *therameeka*

Practise with these words:

corrida   *korreeda*   flamenco   *flamenko*
recomendar   *rekomendar*   catedral   *katedral*

try it out

as if you were there

You go to the tourist office to find out what there is to do on Sundays in Cáceres. Follow the prompts to play your part.

(Greet her and ask what there is to do here)
Pues hay una corrida de toros. ¿Le gustan los toros?
(Say no, then ask if there are any fiestas)
Sí, hay una fiesta de baile regional aquí en la Plaza Mayor.
(Ask what time it starts)
A las diez de la mañana.
(Say, and tonight?)
Hay cines, un concierto de música clásica, también hay fuegos artificiales a las once.
(Find out where you can get tickets for the concert)
Aquí. Son de doce euros.

linkup

likes, dislikes & preferences

For likes and dislikes, Spanish uses the idea of 'pleasing'.

Me gusta la música. I like music. (literally, Music pleases me)

So, for dislikes you say:

No me gusta el vino. I don't like wine.

And when what you like is plural, you say:

Me gustan las películas españolas. I like Spanish films.

You can show preferences very simply:

Me gusta el cine, pero prefiero el teatro. I like the cinema but I prefer the theatre.

And you can express stronger feelings:

Me gusta mucho. I like it a lot.
Me encanta el flamenco. I adore flamenco.
No me gusta nada. I don't like it at all.

To say what you like doing, use me gusta followed by the infinitive of the verb:

Me gusta jugar al fútbol. I like playing football.
No me gusta ir de compras. I don't like going shopping.

can & can't

If you want to find out what you can and can't do in a place, there's a very simple formula using se puede followed by the infinitive of the verb:

¿Se puede pescar aquí? Can you go fishing here?

This is a form of the verb poder, but it's best remembered as a very handy little phrase, as in these examples:

¿Se puede aparcar en la plaza? Can you park in the square?

And you may get a response using no se puede:

No se puede bañar en el río. You can't swim in the river.

Emergencies

reporting crime

Report any incidents to the nearest police station immediately. They will be able to issue you with a crime number for insurance purposes. There are three types of police. The **Policía Local**, in blue and white uniforms, deal with any crimes in their region, especially smaller offences (such as bag-snatching). The **Policía Nacional**, in brown uniforms, deal with more serious crimes such as robberies and rape; they also guard key government buildings. The **Guardia Civil**, in green uniforms, deal with security on the roads and collect on-the-spot fines for traffic offences. Do not confuse the police with the armed security guards outside companies, banks and in the metro.

illness

If you fall ill, go to the nearest **farmacia** (chemist's), where they will recommend the appropriate treatment. In most areas, there is a **farmacia de guardia** (emergency chemist's) open 24 hours. Check in the local papers, tourist office or outside any chemist's for the list showing the details of the nearest one. If the matter is more serious, they will refer you to the nearest **ambulatorio** (doctor's clinic). You will probably have to pay, but should be able to claim the cost back on insurance (make sure they give you all the necessary paperwork). Private treatment is readily available, especially in tourist areas. Look for the sign **Clínica** or **Doctor**.

The **Urgencias** (casualty department) in any hospital should be able to deal with most emergencies.

EU nationals with a European Health Insurance Card are entitled to free emergency medical care in Spain (available from UK post offices, or online: **www.dh.gov.uk/travellers**).

Tap water is safe to drink on the mainland, but can taste salty, so you might prefer bottled mineral water.

breakdowns

There are special SOS phones on autopistas and autovías, or just dial 112. If you bring your own car, it is a good idea to get hold of a green card from your insurance company before leaving home. If you are a member of an automobile club, it might have a reciprocal agreement with RACE (Real Automóvil Club de España): See **www.race.es**.

making phone calls

Public phones can often be found inside bars or cafeterias. Most take coins or a **tarjeta telefónica** (phone card), available as €5 and €10 cards from estancos. Some also accept foreign credit cards.

post offices

Main post offices (**Correos**) accept **apartado de correos** (poste restante) mail for a small fee. You can also buy stamps

(**sellos**) in an **estanco**. Post boxes are yellow, with separate slots for local post, **Resto de España** (rest of Spain) and **Internacional** (abroad).

travellers with disabilities

Facilities for travellers with disabilities are improving. New buildings and most large hotels now have full access. For smaller hotels and public places you will usually find entry and toilet access is provided, but it is worth checking before you arrive. Look for information under **minusválidos** or **discapacitados**.

useful telephone numbers

Emergencies 112
Police 091
Ambulance 061
Fire brigade 080
Directory enquiries 11820
International directory enquiries 11825

phrasemaker

emergency phrases
you may say ...

Help!	¡Socorro!	*sokorro*
Watch out!	¡Cuidado!	*kweedado*
Hello there!	¡Oiga!	*oyga*
Excuse me!	¡Por favor!	*por fabor*
Can you help me?	¿Me puede ayudar?	*meh pwedeh aeeoodar*
Where is the nearest ...	¿Dónde está ... más cercana?	*dondeh esta ... mas therkana*
police station?	la comisaría	*la komeesareea*
chemist's?	la farmacia	*la farmatheea*
petrol station?	la gasolinera	*la gasoleenera*
Where is the nearest ...	¿Dónde está ... más cercano?	*dondeh esta ... mas therkano*
hospital?	el hospital	*el ospeetal*
telephone?	el teléfono	*el telefono*
garage?	el garaje	*el gara*cheh*
I need ...	Necesito ...	*netheseeto*
a doctor.	un médico.	*oon medeeko*
an ambulance.	una ambulancia.	*oona amboolantheea*
It's urgent.	Es urgente.	*es oor*chenteh*
Do you speak English?	¿Habla usted inglés?	*abla oosteh eengles*
I'd like to speak to a dentist.	Quisiera hablar con un dentista.	*keeseeeyera ablar kon oon denteesta*
Leave me alone!	¡Déjeme en paz!	*de*chameh en path*
I'll call the police!	¡Voy a llamar a la policía!	*boy a yamar a la poleetheea*

talking to a doctor or a dentist

you may say ...

I'd like an appointment.	Quisiera una cita.	*keeseeyera oona theeta*
My ... hurts.	Me duele ...	*meh dweleh*
throat	la garganta.	*la garganta*
neck	el cuello.	*el kweyo*
head	la cabeza.	*la kabetha*
tooth	esta muela.	*esta mwela*
My eyes/feet hurt.	Me duelen los ojos/pies.	*meh dwelen los o*chos/peeyes*
It hurts a lot/a bit/here.	Me duele mucho/un poco/aquí.	*meh dweleh mootcho/oon poko/akee*
I've been sick.	He vomitado.	*eh bomeetado*
I feel sick.	Tengo ganas de vomitar.	*tengo ganas de bomeetar*
I can't ...	No puedo ...	*no pwedo*
move my arm.	mover el brazo.	*mober el bratho*
breathe properly.	respirar bien.	*respeerar beeyen*
I've cut/burnt myself.	Me he cortado/quemado.	*meh eh kortado/kemado*
I've lost a filling.	He perdido un empaste.	*eh perdeedo oon empasteh*
I have ...	Tengo ...	*tengo*
asthma.	asma.	*asma*
high/low blood pressure.	la tensión arterial alta/baja.	*la tenseeon artereeal alta/ba*cha*
arthritis.	artritis.	*artreetees*
I'm ...	Soy ...	*soy*
allergic to antibiotics.	alérgico/a a los antibióticos.	*aler*cheeko/a a las anteebeeoteekos*
diabetic.	diabético/a.	*deeabeteeko/a*
HIV positive.	seropositivo/a.	*seroposeeteebo/a*
I'm pregnant.	Estoy embarazada.	*estoy embarathada*
I wear contacts.	Llevo lentillas	*yebo lenteeyas*
My son/daughter has a temperature.	Mi hijo/hija tiene fiebre.	*mee ee*cho/ee*cha teeyeneh feeyebreh*
He/she is allergic to ...	Es alérgico/a a ...	*es aler*cheeko/a a*

you may hear ...

¿Dónde le duele?	*dondeh leh **dwe**leh*	Where does it hurt?
¿Le duele mucho?	*leh **dwe**leh **moo**tcho*	Does it hurt a lot?
Desnúdese, por favor.	*des**noo**deseh por fa**bor***	Please undress.
¿Toma algún medicamento?	*toma al**goon** medeeka**men**to*	Are you on medication?
¿Es alérgico/a a algo?	*es a**ler***cheeko/a a **al**go*	Are you allergic to anything?
No es grave.	*no es **gra**beh*	It's not serious.
Tiene un hueso roto.	*tee**eye**neh oon **we**so **ro**to*	You have a broken bone.
Hay que operar.	*aee keh ope**rar***	You need an operation.
Es ...	*es*	It's ...
una fractura.	*oona frak**too**ra*	a fracture.
un tirón.	*oon tee**ron***	a pulled muscle.
una intoxicación alimentaria.	*oona eentoxeeka**theeon** aleemen**ta**reea*	food poisoning.
Esta es una receta.	*esta es **oo**na re**the**ta*	This is a prescription.
¿Tiene una tarjeta del seguro de enfermedad europeo?	*tee**eye**neh **oo**na tar***che**ta del se**goo**ro de enferme**da** eooro**pe**o*	Do you have a European Health Insurance Card?
Voy a empastar/ sacar la muela.	*boy a empas**tar**/sa**kar** la **mwe**la*	I'm going to fill/take out the tooth.
Debe ...	***de**beh*	You must ...
descansar.	*deskan**sar***	rest.
dormir.	*dor**meer***	sleep.
beber mucha agua.	*be**ber moo**tcha agwa*	drink lots of water.
No debe ...	*no **de**beh*	You mustn't ...
salir.	*sa**leer***	go out.
levantarse.	*leban**tar**seh*	get up.

at the chemist's

you may say ...

Do you have anything for ...	¿Tiene algo para ...	*teeyeneh algo para ...*
hayfever?	la fiebre del heno?	*la feeyebreh del eno*
a headache?	el dolor de cabeza?	*el dolor deh kabetha*
indigestion?	la indigestion?	*la eendee*chesteeon*
sunburn?	las quemaduras de sol?	*las kemadooras de sol*
bites?	las picaduras?	*las peekadooras*
travel sickness?	el mareo?	*el mareo*
I've got ...	Estoy ...	*estoy*
a cold.	constipado/a.	*konsteepado/a*
constipation.	estreñido/a.	*estrenyeedo/a*
I've got ...	Tengo ...	*tengo*
diarrhoea.	diarrea.	*deearrea*
a cough.	tos.	*tos*
flu.	gripe.	*greepeh*
Do you have ...	¿Tiene ...	*teeyeneh*
aspirin?	aspirina?	*aspeereena*
painkillers?	calmantes?	*kalmantes*
aftersun lotion?	aftersun?	*aftersoon*
antihistamine?	antihistamínicos?	*antee-eestameeneekos*
baby food?	comida para bebés?	*komeeda para bebes*
condoms?	condones?	*kondones*
cough mixture?	un jarabe?	*oon *charabeh*
nappies?	pañales?	*panyales*
plasters?	tiritas?	*teereetas*
a laxative?	un laxante?	*oon laksanteh*
insect repellent?	repelente contra insectos?	*repelenteh kontra eensektos*

I need some ...	Necesito ...	*netheseeto*
shampoo.	champú.	*champoo*
toothpaste.	pasta de dientes.	*pasta deh deeyentes*
shaving cream.	crema de afeitar.	*krema deh afaytar*
sun lotion.	bronceador.	*brontheador*
contact lens solution.	solución para lentillas.	*solootheeon para lenteeyas*
sanitary towels.	compresas.	*kompresas*
tampons.	tampones.	*tampones*
How often do I have to take it?	¿Con qué frecuencia la tomo?	*kon keh frekwentheea la tomo*
Does it have side effects?	¿Tiene efectos secundarios?	*teeyeneh efektos sekoondareeos*

you may hear ...

¿Qué ha comido/ bebido?	*keh a komeedo/ bebeedo*	What have you eaten/drunk?
Tome ...	*tomeh*	Take ...
este jarabe.	*esteh *charabeh*	this syrup.
estas pastillas.	*estas pasteeyas*	these pills.
estos antibióticos.	*estos anteebeeoteekos*	these antibiotics.
Aplíquese esta pomada/crema ...	*apleekeseh esta pomada/krema*	Put on this cream ...
en seguida.	*ensegeeda*	straight away.
una vez al día.	*oona beth al deea*	once a day.
tres veces al día.	*tres bethes al deea*	three times a day.
cada cuatro horas.	*kada kwatro oras*	every four hours.
antes/después de las comidas.	*antes/despwes deh las komeedas*	before/after meals.
Puede causar somnolencia.	*pwedeh kowsar somnolentheea*	May cause drowsiness.
Tráguese sin masticar.	*trageseh seen masteekar*	Swallow without chewing.
Mastique.	*masteekeh*	Chew.

Emergencies

check out 1

You go to see the chemist about your stomach problems.

○ Me duele el estómago.
*meh **dwe**leh el es**to**mago*

- ¿Está estreñida?
*es**ta** estre**nyee**da*

○ No, tengo un poco de diarrea.
*no **ten**go oon **po**ko deh dee**arre**a*

- No es grave. Tome este jarabe cada cuatro horas.
*no es **gra**beh. **to**meh **es**teh *cha**ra**beh **ka**da **kwa**tro **o**ras*

Q Is it serious?
How often should you take the syrup?

parts of the body

ankle	el tobillo	*el to**bee**yo*
arm	el brazo	*el **bra**tho*
back	la espalda	*la es**pal**da*
body	el cuerpo	*el **kwer**po*
chest	el pecho	*el **pe**tcho*
inner/outer ear	el oído/la oreja	*el o**yee**do/la ore*cha*
eyes	los ojos	*los **o***chos*
foot	el pie	*el pee**yeh***
hand	la mano	*la **ma**no*
head	la cabeza	*la ka**be**tha*
hip	la cadera	*la ka**de**ra*
kidneys	los riñones	*los reen**yo**nes*
knee	la rodilla	*la ro**dee**ya*
leg	la pierna	*la pee**yer**na*
nose	la nariz	*la na**reeth***
shoulder	el codo	*el **ko**do*
stomach	el estómago	*el es**to**mago*
thigh	el muslo	*el **moos**lo*

car breakdown

you may say ...

Can you help me?	¿Me puede ayudar?	meh **pwe**deh aeeoo**dar**
I have broken down.	Tengo una avería.	**ten**go **oo**na abe**ree**a
The car has a flat tyre.	El coche tiene un pinchazo.	el **kotch**eh **tee**yeneh oon peen**tcha**tho
The car/engine won't start.	El coche/motor no arranca.	el **ko**tcheh/mo**tor** no a**rran**ka

The ... isn't working.
  battery
  horn
	... no funciona.
	  La batería
	  La bocina
		... no foonthee**o**na
		  la bate**ree**a
		  la bo**thee**na

The lights aren't working.	Las luces no funcionan.	las **loo**thes no foonthee**o**nan
I've run out of petrol.	Estoy sin gasolina.	es**toy** seen gaso**lee**na

I'm ...
  on the N26.
 	
  at kilometre 110.
 	
  15km from ...
	Estoy ...
	  en la carretera N26.
	
	  en el kilómetro ciento diez.
	  a quince kilómetros de ...
		es**toy**
		  en la karre**te**ra **en**eh bayntee**says**
		  en el **kee**lometro thee**yen**to dee**yeth**
		  a **keen**theh **kee**lometros deh

How long will they be?	¿Cuánto tardarán?	**kwan**to tarda**ran**
When will it be ready?	¿Cuándo estará listo?	**kwan**do esta**ra lees**to

you may hear ...

¿Qué le pasa?	keh leh **pa**sa	What's the matter?

¿Cuál es su ...
  mátricula?
 	
  nombre?
	kwal es soo
	  ma**tree**koola
	
	  nombreh
		What's your ...
		  car registration number?
		  name?

Mandaremos a un mecánico ...
  ahora mismo/ en seguida.
  dentro de dos horas.
	manda**re**mos a oon me**kan**eeko
	  a**o**ra **mees**mo/ en se**gee**da
	  dentro deh dos **o**ras
		We'll send a mechanic ...
		  straight away.
		
		  in two hours.

check out 2
You're having car troubles, and phone a mechanic.

○ Buenos días. Tengo una avería.
bwenos deeas. tengo oona abereea

- ¿Dónde está su coche?
dondeh esta soo kotcheh

○ En el kilómetro sesenta y cinco.
en el keelometro sesenta ee theenko

- ¿Qué le pasa?
keh leh pasa

○ El motor no arranca. ¿Me puede ayudar?
el motor no arranka. meh pwedeh aeeoodar

- Sí, ahora mismo.
see aora meesmo

Q You have a flat tyre: true or false?
How soon can you get help?

main car parts

accelerator	el acelerador	*el athelerador*
battery	la batería	*la batereea*
brakes	los frenos	*los frenos*
clutch	el embrague	*el embrageh*
engine	el motor	*el motor*
radiator	el radiador	*el radeeador*
steering wheel	el volante	*el bolanteh*
tyres	los neumáticos	*los neoomateekos*
wheels	las ruedas	*las rwedas*
windows	las ventanillas	*las bentaneeyas*
windscreen	el parabrisas	*el parabreesas*
wipers	el limpiaparabrisas	*el leempeeya-parabreesas*

at the police station

you may say …

I've lost …	He perdido …	*eh perdeedo*
my wallet.	mi cartera.	*mee kartera*
passport.	mi pasaporte.	*mee pasaporteh*
my son/daughter.	a mi hijo/hija.	*a mee ee*cho/ee*cha*
I've had my … stolen.	Me han robado …	*meh an robado*
suitcase	la maleta.	*la maleta*
money	el dinero.	*el deenero*
Our car has been broken into.	Nos han abierto el coche.	*nos an abeeyerto el kotcheh*
I was mugged.	Me han atracado.	*meh an atrakado*
I had an accident.	Tuve un accidente.	*toobeh oon aktheedenteh*
this morning/evening	esta mañana/tarde	*esta manyana/tardeh*
yesterday/last night	ayer/anoche	*aeeyer/anotcheh*
in …	en …	*en*
the street	la calle	*la kayeh*
a shop	una tienda	*oona teeyenda*
It's …	Es …	*es*
big.	grande.	*grandeh*
blue.	azul.	*athool*
expensive.	caro.	*karo*
made of leather.	de cuero.	*deh kwero*
Was a … handed in?	¿Entregaron un/una …?	*entregaron oon/oona*
I think …	Creo …	*krayo*
I don't know.	No sé.	*no seh*

Emergencies

you may hear ...

¿Cuándo?	*kwando*	When?
¿Dónde?	*dondeh*	Where?
¿Qué contenía?	*keh konteneea*	What was in it?
¿Cómo es?	*komo es*	What does it look like?
¿Se ha hecho daño?	*seh a etcho danyo*	Are you hurt?
¿Nombre?	*nombreh*	Name?
El pasaporte, por favor.	*el pasaporteh por fabor*	Your passport, please.
Rellene esta hoja.	*reyeneh esta o*cha*	Fill in this form.
Vuelva mañana.	*bwelba manyana*	Come back tomorrow.
Lo siento, no se ha entregado nada.	*lo seeyento, no seh a entregado nada*	Sorry, nothing has been handed in.

valuables

briefcase	el maletín	*el maleteen*
digital camera	la cámara digital	*la kamara dee*cheetal*
driving licence	el permiso de conducir	*el permeeso deh kondootheer*
handbag	el bolso	*el bolso*
jewellery	las joyas	*las *choyas*
laptop	el láptop	*el laptop*
mobile	el móvil	*el mobeel*
money	el dinero	*el deenero*
MP3 player	el MP3	*el emeh peh tres*
necklace	el collar	*el koyar*
purse	el monedero	*el monedero*
ring	la sortija/ el anillo	*la sortee*chal el aneeyo*
suitcase	la maleta	*la maleta*
watch	el reloj	*el relo*ch*

check out 3

You report your lost wallet.

- ○ He perdido mi cartera.
  eh perdeedo mee kartera

- – ¿Dónde?
  dondeh

- ○ En la calle, creo.
  en la kayeh krayo

- – ¿Cómo es?
  komo es

- ○ Es negro, de cuero.
  es negro deh kwero

- – Rellene esta hoja y vuelva mañana.
  reyeneh esta o*cha ee bwelba manyana

Q Your wallet is red and plastic: true or false?
What do you have to do?

sound check

In Spanish, when **g** is followed by **e** or **i**, it sounds like the 'ch' in the Scottish word 'loch'.

ginebra **cheenebra*   urgente *oor*chenteh*

Practise with these words:

alérgico *aler*cheeko*   general **cheneral*

When **g** is followed by anything else, it is pronounced like the 'g' in 'go'.

garganta *garganta*   garaje *gara*cheh*

Practise with these words:

oiga *oyga*   gracias *gratheeas*
hígado *eegado*   en seguida *en segeeda*

try it out

match it up

Match each of these phrases with the best reply.

1 ¿Me puede ayudar?
2 ¿Qué le pasa?
3 ¡Muchas gracias!
4 ¿Tardarán mucho?
5 ¿Dónde está su coche?

a De nada.
b En la carretera de Madrid.
c Me duelen las muelas.
d Sí, claro.
e No, unos momentos.

as if you were there

You're not feeling well, so you go to a chemist's. Follow the prompts to play your part.

Buenos días.
(Say good morning, then tell her you have sunburn)
¿Le duele la cabeza?
(Say yes, a little, and tell her you've been sick)
Aplíquese esta pomada. Y debe descansar.
(Say thank you very much)
De nada.

linkup

key phrases

saying something hurts

There are two simple ways of saying what's hurting. You can say:

Tengo un dolor de cabeza. I have a headache.
(literally, I have a pain of the head)
Or you can use me duele, which you use in the same way as me gusta:

Me duele la cabeza. My head hurts.
(literally, It hurts to me the head)

Me duelen las piernas. My legs hurt.
(literally, They hurt to me the legs)

possession

The apostrophe s ('s and s') doesn't exist in Spanish, so to express possession or belonging, you change the order of the words:

El apartamento de mi hermano. My brother's flat (literally, the flat of my brother)
El coche de mi amigo. My friend's car.
La casa de mis padres. My parents' house.

The word de is also very useful when linking two other words:

un dolor de cabeza a headache
la camisa de algodón a cotton shirt
la carretera de Madrid the Madrid road

gender

All Spanish nouns (words used for people things and concepts) are either feminine or masculine. The gender of a word affects the form of 'a' and 'the' used before it, and any adjectives used with it.

Masculine words usually end in **-o**: teléfono, estanco (telephone, tobacconist's).

Feminine words usually end in **-a**: revista, farmacia (magazine, chemist's).

'a' & 'the': the articles

	masculine	feminine	masc. plural	fem. plural
a, some	un	una	unos	unas
the	el	la	los	las

Some examples:

una cerveza a beer	un vaso a glass
la camisa the shirt	el vestido the dress
las camisas the shirts	los vestidos the dresses

When learning a new word, it also is useful to learn whether it is masculine or feminine. So, for example, instead of just learning the words cereza (cherry) and melón (melon), learn una/la cereza, and un/el melón.

singular & plural

When you are talking about more than one person or thing, you normally add an **-s** to the word if it ends in any of the following vowels: **-a**, **-e**, or **-o**.

una pera one pear	dos peras two pears
un plátano one banana	dos plátanos two bananas
un albaricoque one apricot	dos albaricoques two apricots

Language **Builder**

Add **es** if it ends in a consonant or any other letter:

un señor one gentleman	dos señores two gentlemen
un limón one lemon	dos limones two lemons

talking to people

In Spanish you use a different word for 'you' depending on how many people you are talking to and how well you know them.

For example, you use:

usted to someone you don't know well or an older person (formal)

tú to a friend, member of the family, or younger person (informal).

Here are the different ways you would ask 'Do you speak English?':

¿Habla (usted) inglés? (to one person, formal)

¿Hablan (ustedes) inglés? (to more than one person, formal)

¿Hablas (tú) inglés? (to one person, informal)

¿Habláis (vosotros) inglés? (to more than one person, informal. If they are all female, use vosotr**as**)

If in doubt, it is always safer to be polite and use the formal form (usted or ustedes).

verbs

The endings of Spanish verbs change according to who does the action and when. Look at the example for the verb hablar (to speak), on the next page. These endings are for regular verbs ending in **-ar**.

(For the different meanings of 'you', see 'talking to people', above)

hablar: to speak	
(yo) hablo	I speak
(tú) hablas	you speak
(él/ella; usted) habla	he/she/it speaks; you speak
(nosotros) hablamos	we speak
(vosotros/as) habláis	you speak
(ellos/ellas; ustedes) hablan	they speak; you speak

There are two other common patterns of verbs: those ending in **-er** and those ending in **-ir**. The following examples show the endings of regular verbs of these types.

comer: to eat	
(yo) como	I eat
(tú) comes	you eat
(él/ella; usted) come	he/she/it eats; you eat
(nosotros) comemos	we eat
(vosotros/as) coméis	you eat
(ellos/ellas; ustedes) comen	they eat; you eat

vivir: to live	
(yo) vivo	I live
(tú) vives	you live
(él/ella; usted) vive	he/she/it lives; you live
(nosotros) vivimos	we live
(vosotros/as) vivís	you live
(ellos/ellas; ustedes) viven	they live; you live

Verbs that follow the patterns above are called regular verbs. However, many of the common verbs are irregular verbs and must be learnt individually.

Language **Builder**

adjectives

Adjectives 'agree' with the nouns they describe, so they have different endings for masculine and feminine, singular and plural words. Often adjectives end in **-o** for masculine or **-a** for feminine, and add an **-s** for the plural of both.

singular
un museo modern**o** a modern museum
una iglesia modern**a** a modern church

plural
manzanas amarill**as** yellow apples (manzana is feminine)
pimientos amarill**os** yellow peppers (pimiento is masculine)

Some adjectives, including those ending in **-e** and most of those ending in a consonant, only have one singular form, and add an **-s** or an **-es** in the plural:

una manzana verd**e**, manzanas verd**es** a green apple, green apples
un pimiento verd**e**, pimientos verd**es** a green pepper, green peppers
una camisa azu**l**, camisas azul**es** a blue shirt, blue shirts
un coche azu**l**, coches azul**es** a blue car, blue cars

Note that unlike in English, adjectives generally come after the noun. However. there are some common exceptions which always come before the noun:

alguno (any, some)	otro (other)
bueno (good)	poco (not much, few)
cada (every, all)	primero (first)
malo (bad)	todo (every, all)
mucho (much, many)	último (last)

questions

There are two easy ways to ask a question. You can change the word order of a statement:
El mercado está cerca. The market is close.
¿Está cerca el mercado? Is the market close?

Or you can use the same order, but with a question intonation:
Tiene manzanas. You have some apples.
¿Tiene manzanas? Do you have any apples?
The rise in your voice turns the sentence into a question, and the context in which you are speaking will usually prevent any confusion.

Some useful question words:
¿**Dónde** está la catedral? Where is the cathedral?
¿**Cuánto** vale? How much does it cost?
¿**Quién** vive aquí? Who lives here?
¿**Qué** color prefieres? Which colour do you prefer?
¿**Por qué** haces eso? Why are you doing that?
¿**Cuándo** empieza la película? When does the film begin?
¿**A qué** hora termina? What time does it finish?

talking about possession

De (of) is used to show possession:
la maleta de Anna Anna's suitcase

There are special words for personal possession. They are adjectives (see above), so they all 'agree' with the nouns they refer to:
mi reloj my watch
mis gafas my glasses

	singular	plural
my	mi	mis
your	su	sus
	tu	tus
	vuestro/a	vuestros/as
his/her/its	su	sus
our	nuestro/a	nuestros/as
their	su	sus

this, that, these, those

These words behave like adjectives so they have different forms, depending on what they refer to:

este melón/estos melones this melon/these melons
esta sandía/estas sandías this watermelon/these watermelons
ese melón/esos melones that melon/those melons
esa sandía/esas sandías that watermelon/those watermelons

things you like: gustar

To talk about what you like and dislike in Spanish, use the phrases me gusta and me gustan:

Me gusta el vino tinto, no me gusta el vino blanco. I like red wine, I don't like white wine.

Me gustan las alcachofas, no me gustan las berenjenas. I like artichokes, I don't like aubergines.

What the Spanish literally means is 'Red wine is pleasing to me.' and 'Artichokes are pleasing to me.' So, when you are talking about one thing, use the singular form me gust**a**, and when you are talking about more than one thing, use the plural form me gust**an**. Try to remember that the verb gustar means 'to please', and take it from there.

pronouns

In Spanish you don't generally need to use a pronoun (I, you, he etc.) in front of a verb, as the ending of the verb makes it clear who is being referred to.

Hablo inglés. I speak English (instead of Yo hablo inglés)
¿Tiene aceite? Do you have any oil? (instead of ¿Tiene usted aceite?)

the two verbs 'to be'

There are two verbs meaning 'to be' in Spanish, which can be quite confusing. They are ser and estar.

Estar is used for temporary states and for locations. For example:
¿Dónde está la Plaza Mayor? Where is the Main Square?
Está al final de la calle. It's at the end of the street.
Está enfermo. He is ill.
Otherwise ser is used:
¿Cómo es la Plaza Mayor? What is the Main Square like?
Es magnífica. It's magnificent.
Soy inglés. I am English.

They are both irregular:

	ser	estar
yo	soy	estoy
tú	eres	estás
él/ella/usted	es	está
nosotros/as	somos	estamos
vosotros/as	sois	estáis
ellos/as/ustedes	son	están

Answers

Bare Necessities.......

check out
1 where you're from; Mexico
2 afternoon; €1.60
3 €1.46; your passport

question time
1 Buenas tardes.
2 ¿A qué hora abren?
3 Le presento a mi esposa.
4 ¿Dónde está el Hotel San Jorge?
5 ¿Quiere repetir eso?
6 ¿Tiene gasolina sin plomo?
7 ¿Cuánto es?
8 ¿Hay servicios?

as if you were there
Por favor.
por fabor
Buenos días.
bwenos deeas
¿Dónde está el banco?
dondeh esta el banko
¿A qué hora cierran?
a keh ora theeyeran
Muchas gracias
mootchas gratheeas
Adiós
adeeyos

Getting Around.........

check out
1 the end of the street on the left; false, 500m
2 a small three-door; €50
3 unleaded; 30km (approximately)
4 false, platform 9; 20 minutes

picture this
1e 2d 3f 4c 5b 6a

crossed lines
1 d; a; c; e; b
2 d; a; e; b; c

as if you were there
Buenas tardes. ¿Hay autobuses para Salamanca?
bwenas tardes, aee owtobooses para salamanka
¿A qué hora sale el autobús?
a keh ora saleh el owtoboos
¿Cuánto tarda?
kwanto tarda
Dos billetes de ida y vuelta.
dos beeyetes deh eeda ee bwelta

Somewhere to Stay.....

check out
1 false, double; one
2 false, it's €9; for your passport and to fill in a form
3 you can't work the TV, and there's no hot water
4 true (€118); credit card

all the 'a's
1 habitación
2 reserva
3 llave
4 cama
5 pasaporte
6 ascensor
7 escalera
8 restaurante
9 desayuno
10 cena
11 ducha
12 agua

in the mix
m; j; c; d; n; f; g; l; i; b; k; h; a; e

as if you were there

Buenos dias. Quiero pagar la cuenta.

bwenos deeas, keeyero pagar la kwenta

La cuarenta y siete.

la kwarenta ee seeyeteh

Con tarjeta de crédito.

kon tar*cheta deh kredeeto

Gracias, adiós.

gratheeas adeeyos

Buying Things..........

check out
1 peaches; €5.30
2 true; size 50

in the mix
1 zumo	2 plátano
3 jamón	4 melocotón
5 alcachofa	6 queso
7 huevo	8 sardina
9 naranja	10 cereza

match it up
1d 2f 3a 4c 5e 6b

as if you were there

Cien gramos de chorizo y doscientos gramos de jamón serrano.

theeyen gramos deh choreetho ee dostheeyentos gramos deh *chamon serrano

¿Tiene pan?

teeyeneh pan?

Una barra grande.

oona barra grandeh

Nada más, gracias. ¿Cuánto es?

nada mas gratheeas. kwanto es

Aquí tiene. Gracias, adiós.

akee teeyeneh gratheeas adeeyos

Café Life.................

check out
1 pineapple and orange juice, (iced) lemon
2 brandy
3 squid and prawns

allergies
chorizo, empanadillas de carne, aceitunas

as if you were there

Buenas tardes. Pónganos una cerveza, un vermú y un vino blanco, por favor.

bwenas tardes. ponganos oona therbetha, oon bermoo ee oon beeno blanko por fabor

¿Qué tapas tienen?

keh tapas teeyenen

Una ración de jamón serrano, boquerones, chorizo y tortilla.

oona ratheeon deh *chamon serrano bokerones choreetho ee torteeya

¿Cuánto es?

kwanto es

Eating Out...............

check out
1 false, to drink
2 fish soup and a salad; besugo al horno (baked sea bream)

3 yes, Visa and Mastercard

match it up
1d 2f 3a 4e 5c 6b

as if you were there
Buenas tardes. Una mesa para dos, por favor.

bwenas tardes. oona mesa para dos por fabor

Un vaso de vino tinto y un fino.

oon baso deh beeno teento ee oon feeno

¿Cómo son las 'langostas a la santanderina'?

komo son las langostas a la santandereena?

Dos langostas a la santanderina, y una sopa de ajo y una ensalada.

dos langostas a la santandereena ee oona sopa deh a*cho ee oona ensalada

¡Está muy buena!

esta mooee bwena

No gracias, la cuenta por favor.

no gratheeas la kwenta por fabor.

Entertainment..........

check out
1 the New Cathedral, the Old Cathedral, the Roman bridge; true
2 false, about 11pm; no, it's free
3 €24

as if you were there
Buenos días. ¿Qué se puede hacer aquí?

bwenos deeas. keh seh pwedeh ather akee

No. ¿Hay fiestas?

no. aee feeyestas

¿A qué hora empieza?

a keh ora empeeyetha

¿Y esta noche?

ee esta notcheh

¿Dónde se compran las entradas para el concierto?

dondeh seh kompran las entradas para el kontheeyerto

Emergencies............

check out
1 no; every four hours
2 false, the engine won't start; straight away
3 false, it's black and leather; fill in the form and come back tomorrow

match it up
1 d; 2 c; 3 a; 4 e; 5 b

as if you were there
Buenos días, tengo quemaduras de sol.

bwenos deeas tengo kemadooras de sol

Sí, un poco, y he vomitado.

see oon poko ee eh bomeetado

Muchas gracias.

mootchas gratheeas

A

about, more or less más o menos *mas o menos*
abroad extranjero *estran*chero*
adult adulto/a *adoolto*
afternoon nap siesta, la *seeyesta*
afternoon snack merienda, la *mereeyenda*
afternoon/evening tarde, la *tardeh*
after-sun lotion after-sun, el *aftersoon*
agency agencia, la *a*chentheea*
air aire, el *aeereh*
air conditioning aire acondicionado, el *aeereh akondeetheeonado*
airport aeropuerto, el *ayeropwerto*
all todo/a *todo/a*
allergic alérgico/a *aler*cheeko/a*
almond almendra, la *almendra*
altogether en total *en total*
ambulance ambulancia, la *amboolantheea*
anchovy anchoa, la/boquerón, el *antchoa/bokeron*
angler fish rape, el *rapeh*
anis anís, el *anees*
ankle tobillo, el *tobeeyo*
antibiotics antibióticos, los *anteebeeoteekos*
antihistamine antihistamínico, el *antee'eestameeneeko*
anything else? ¿algo más? *algo mas*
apartment, flat apartamento, el *apartamento*
aperitif aperitivo, el *apereeteebo*
apple manzana, la *manthana*
to apply aplicar *apleekar*
apricot albaricoque, el *albareekokeh*
arm brazo, el *bratho*
A-road autovía, la *owtobeea*
to arrive llegar *yegar*
art gallery galería de arte, la *galereea deh arteh*
artichoke alcachofa, la *alkatchofa*
ashtray cenicero, el *theneethero*
asparagus espárragos, los *esparragos*
aspirin aspirina, la *aspeereena*
assorted variados/as *bareeados*
asthma asma, el *asma*
aubergine berenjena, la *beren*chena*
autumn otoño, el *otonyo*
avocado aguacate, el *agwakateh*

B

back espalda, la *espalda*
bacon bacon, el *be'eekon*
bag bolsa, la *bolsa*
baked in the oven al horno *al orno*
balcony balcón, el *balkon*

ball pelota, la *pelota*
banana plátano, el *platano*
bank banco, el *banko*
bar taberna, la *taberna*
bar tasca, la *taska*
bar/pub cervecería, la *therbethereea*
barbecue brasa, la *brasa*
basement sótano, el *sotano*
bathroom baño, el *banyo*
battered, breaded and fried rebozado/a *rebothado/a*
battery pila, la *peela* (car) batería, la *batereea*
to be estar, ser *estar, ser*
beach playa, la *playa*
beans alubias, las/judías, las *aloobeeas/*choodeeas*
  broad beans habas, las *abas*
  butter beans alubias blancas, las *aloobeeas blankas*
  haricot beans habichuelas, las/judías blancas, las *abeetchwelas/*choodeeas blankas*
  red kidney beans alubias pintas, las *aloobeeas peentas*
bed cama, la *kama*
  double cama de matrimonio, la *kama deh matreemoneeo*
  single cama individual, la *cama eendeebeedwal*
bed and breakfast casa de huéspedes, la *kasa deh wespedes*
beef carne de vaca, la *karneh deh baka*
beer (bottled) cerveza, la *therbetha* (draught) caña, la *kanya*
beetroot remolacha, la *remolatcha*
belt cinturón, el *theentooron*
big grande *grandeh*
bike bicicleta, la *beetheekleta*
bill cuenta, la *kwenta*
black negro/a *negro/a*
black pudding morcilla, la *mortheeya*
blackberries moras, las *moras*
blanket manta, la *manta*
blind persiana, la *perseeana*
blouse blusa, la *bloosa*
blue azul *athool*
boar jabalí, el **chabalee*
boarding house pensión, la *penseeon*
boat barca, la *barka*
body cuerpo, el *kwerpo*
boiled hervido/a *erbeedo/a*
bone hueso, el *weso*
book libro, el *leebro*
to book reservar *reserbar*
boot bota, la *bota*
bottle botella, la *boteya*

bracelet pulsera, la *poolsera*
brain seso, el *seso*
brandy coñac, el *konyak*
bread pan, el *pan*
breaded empanado/a *empanado/a*
breakdown avería, la *abereea*
breakfast desayuno, el *desayoono*
bridge puente, el *pwenteh*
briefcase maletín, el *maleteen*
broccoli brócoli, el *brokolee*
broken roto/a *roto/a*
brown marrón *marron*
bull toro, el *toro*
bullfight corrida de toros, la *korreeda deh toros*
bullfighting toros los *toros*
bun (sweet) magdalena, la *madalena*
bus autobús, el *owtoboos*
bus station estación de autobuses, la *estatheeon deh owtobooses*
business negocio, el *negotheeo*
but pero *pero*
butcher's carnicería, la *karneetheereea*
butter mantequilla, la *mantekeeya*
button botón, el *boton*
to buy comprar *komprar*

C

cabbage berza, la/col, la/repollo, el *bertha/kol/repoyo*
cable car teleférico, el *telefereeko*
cake pastel, el *pastel*
cake shop pastelería, la *pastelereea*
campsite camping, el *kampeeng*
to be able to poder *poder*
cannelloni canelones, los *kanelones*
car coche, el *cotcheh*
carafe garrafa, la *garrafa*
caravan caravana, la *karabana*
card tarjeta, la *tar*cheta*
carnival carnaval, el *karnabal*
carrot zanahoria, la *thanaoreea*
cash dinero en metálico, el *deenero en metaleeko*
casserole cacerola, la *katherola*
cassette cinta, la *theenta*
castle castillo, el *kasteeyo*
cathedral catedral, la *katedral*
cauliflower coliflor, la *koleeflor*
celery apio, el *apeeo*
centre centro, el *thentro*
town centre centro ciudad, el *thentro theeooda*
ceramics cerámica, la *therameeka*
chair silla, la *seeya*
champagne champán, el *champan*
to change cambiar *kambeear*

changing rooms vestuarios, los *bestooareeos*
to chat charlar *charlar*
cheap barato/a *barato/a*
cheese queso, el *keso*
chemist's farmacia, la *farmatheea*
emergency chemist's farmacia de guardia, la *farmatheea deh gwardeea*
cherry cereza, la *theretha*
chest pecho, el *petcho*
chestnut castaña, la *kastanya*
chicken pollo, el *poyo*
chickpeas garbanzos, los *garbanthos*
chicory endivias, las *endeebeeas*
child niño/a *neenyo/a*
chilli guindilla, la *geendeeya*
chips, crisps patatas fritas, las *patatas freetas*
chocolate hot chocolate, el *chokolateh*
chop, cutlet chuleta, la *chooleta*
church iglesia, la *eegleseea*
cider sidra, la *seedra*
cigar puro, el *pooro*
cigarette cigarrillo, el *theegarreeyo*
cinema cine, el *theeneh*
circle (in theatre) anfiteatro, el *anfeeteatro*
clam almeja, la *alme*cha*
clear soup caldo, el *kaldo*
climbing alpinismo, el *alpeeneesmo*
cloakroom guardarropa, el *gwardarropa*
close cerca *therka*
to close cerrar *therrar*
closed cerrado *therrado*
coach autocar, el *owtokar*
coat abrigo, el *abreego*
cod bacalao, el *bakalao*
coffee café, el *kafeh*
black café solo, el *kafeh solo*
Irish café irlandés *kafeh eerlandes*
creamy white café con leche, el *kafeh kon letcheh*
decaffeinated café descafeinado, el *kafeh deskafeh'eenado*
iced café con hielo, el *kafeh kon eeyelo*
small white café cortado, el *kafeh kortado*
cold frío/a *freeo/a*
I have a cold estoy constipado/a *estoy konsteepado/a*
colleague colega, el/la *kolega*
colour color, el *kolor*
commission charge comisión, la *komeeseeon*

complaint book libro de reclamaciones, el *leebro deh reklamatheeones*
concert concierto, el *kontheeyerto*
condom condón, el *kondon*
constipated estreñido/a *estrenyeedo/a*
contact lenses lentillas, las *lenteeyas*
corner esquina, la *eskeena*
cotton algodón, el *algodon*
cough tos, la *tos*
cough mixture jarabe, el **charabeh*
country país, el *paees*
courgette calabacín, el *kalabatheen*
course (meal) plato, el *plato*
cover charge cubierto, el *koobeeyerto*
crab cangrejo, el *kangre*cho*
cream nata, la/crema, la *nata/krema*
cream cheese requesón, el *rekeson*
credit card tarjeta de crédito, la *tar*cheta deh kredeeto*
crème caramel flan, el *flan*
crisps, chips patatas fritas, las *patatas freetas*
croquette croqueta, la *kroketa*
to cross cruzar *kroothar*
crossroads cruce, el *krootheh*
croutons picatostes, los *peekatostes*
cucumber pepino, el *pepeeno*
cup taza, la *tatha*
curd cheese queso fresco, el *keso fresko*
custard natillas, las *nateeyas*
custard apple chirimoya, la *cheereemoya*
cuttlefish sepia, la *sepeea*

D

to dance bailar *baeelar*
dance hall sala de baile, la *sala deh baeeleh*
daughter hija, la *ee*cha*
day día, el *deea*
day after tomorrow pasado mañana *pasado manyana*
day before yesterday anteayer *ante'aeeyer*
deep fried, in batter a la romana *a la romana*
delicatessen charcutería, la *charkootereea*
delicious rico/a *reeko/a*
dentist dentista, el *denteesta*
department sección, la *sektheeon*
dessert postre, el *postreh*
to develop (film) revelar *rebelar*
diabetic diabético/a *deeabeteeko/a*
diarrhoea diarrea, la *deearrea*
dinner cena, la *thena*
disco discoteca, la *deeskoteka*

dish plato, el *plato*
dish of the day plato del día, el *plato del deea*
district barrio, el *barreeo*
doctor médico/a *medeeko*
doughnut buñuelo, el *boonywelo*
dozen docena, la *dothena*
dress vestido, el *besteedo*
to drink beber *beber*
drink bebida, la *bebeeda*
cold drink refresco, el *refresko*
driving licence permiso de conducir, el *permeeso deh kondootheer*
dry seco/a *seko/a*
duck pato, el *pato*
dustbin cubo de la basura, el *koobo deh la basoora*

E

ear oído, el *oeedo*
outer ear oreja, la *ore*cha*
earrings pendientes, los *pendeeyentes*
eggs huevos, los *webos*
boiled eggs huevos pasados por agua, los *webos pasados por agwa*
hard boiled eggs huevos cocidos/duros, los *webos kotheedos/dooros*
poached eggs huevos escalfados, los *webos eskalfados*
scrambled eggs huevos revueltos, los *webos rebweltos*
elbow codo, el *kodo*
end final, el *feenal*
endive escarola, la *eskarola*
engine motor, el *motor*
English inglés/esa *eengles*
entrance entrada, la *entrada*
environment ambiente, el *ambeeyenteh*
exchange rate cambio, el *kambeeo*
excuse me! ¡perdone! *perdoneh*
exhibition exposición, la *esposeetheeon*
exit salida, la *saleeda*
eyes ojos, los *o*chos*

F

fair feria *fereea*
far away lejos *bastanteh le*chos*
fashion moda, la *moda*
fast/quick rápido *rapeedo/a*
feet pies, los *peeyes*
fennel hinojo, el *eeno*cho*
festival feria, la/fiesta, la/el festival *fereea/feeyesta/festeebal*
fever fiebre, la *feeyebreh*
fig higo, el *eego*
to fill (a tooth) empastar *empastar*
to fill in (a form) rellenar *reyenar*
fill it up with … (petrol) llénelo de *yenelo deh*

144

illet filete, el *feeleteh*
ilm (cinema/camera) película, la *peleekoola*
  black and white film película en blanco y negro *peleekoola en blanko ee negro*
inger dedo, el *dedo*
ireworks fuegos artificiales, los *fwegos arteefeetheeales*
irst primero/a *preemerola*
irst floor planta baja, la *planta ba*cha*
ish pescado, el *peskado*
to fish pescar *peskar*
flavour sabor, el *sabor*
floor piso, el *peeso*
floor planta, la *planta*
football fútbol, el *footbol*
for para *para*
form ficha, la *feetcha*
free (price) gratuito/a *gratweetola*
free (available) libre *leebreh*
fresh fresco/a *freskola*
fried frito/a *freetola*
fritters churros, los *choorros*
from de *deh*
fruiterer's shop frutería, la *frootereea*
full completo/a *kompletola*
full board pensión completa, la *penseeon kompleta*

G

game (ent.) juego, el **chwego*
  (food) caza, la *katha* **(football)** partido, el *parteedo*
garlic ajo, el *a*cho*
gentlemen caballeros, los *kabayeros*
to get up levantarse *lebantarseh*
gherkin pepinillo, el *pepeeneeyo*
gin ginebra, la **cheenebra*
gin and tonic gintonic, el *yeentoneek*
to give dar *dar*
glass vaso, el *baso* **(wine)** copa, la *kopa*
gloves guantes, los *gwantes*
golf club/course palo/campo de golf, el *palo/kampo deh golf*
good bueno/a *bweno*
good afternoon/evening buenas tardes *bwenas tardes*
good morning buenos días *bwenos deeas*
good night buenas noches *bwenas notches*
goodbye adiós *adeeyos*
goose ganso, el *ganso*
grape harvest vendimia, la *bendeemeea*

grapefruit pomelo, el *pomelo*
grapes uvas, las *oobas*
green verde *berdeh*
greengrocer's verdulería, la *berdoolereea*
griddled a la plancha *a la plantcha*
grill parrilla, la *parreeya*
  mixed grill parrillada, la *parreeyada*
grilled a la parrilla *a la parreeya*
grocer's shop tienda de alimentación, la *teeyenda deh aleementatheeon*
groceries comestibles, los *komesteebles*
guide guía, la *geeya*

H

hake merluza, la *merlootha*
half an hour media hora, la *medeea ora*
half board media pensión, la *medeea penseeyon*
half price mitad de precio *meetath deh pretheeo*
ham jamón, el **chamon*
  cured ham jamón serrano, el **chamon serrano*
  boiled ham jamón de York, el **chamon deh york*
hand mano, la *mano*
handbag bolso, el *bolso*
hardware store ferretería, la *ferretereea*
hare liebre, la *leeyebreh*
hat sombrero, el *sombrero*
to have tener *tener*
hazelnut avellana, la *abeyana*
head cabeza, la *kabetha*
headache dolor de cabeza, el *dolor deh kabetha*
hello! ¡hola! *ola*
help! ¡socorro! *sokorro*
to help ayudar *aeeoodar*
hen gallina, la *gayeena*
her su *soo*
herbs hierbas, las *eeyerbas*
here aquí *akee*
here you are aquí tiene/tenga *akee teeyeneh/tenga*
herring arenque, el *arenkeh*
hip cadera, la *kadera*
to hire alquilar *alkeelar*
hire car coche de alquiler, el *kotcheh deh alkeelar*
holiday vacaciones, las *bakatheeones*
Holy Week, Easter Semana Santa, la *semana santa*
honey miel, la *meeyel*

hors d'oeuvres entremeses, los
  entremeses
hot caliente *kaleeyenteh*
hotel hotel, el *otel*
hotel, residence hostal, el *ostal*
hour hora, la *ora*
how long does it take? ¿cuánto tarda?
  kwanto tarda
how much? ¿cuánto? *kwanto*
how much are they? ¿cuánto son?
  kwanto son
how much is it? ¿cuánto es? *kwanto es*
to hurt doler *doler*
  hurt, it hurts duele *dweleh*
husband marido, el *mareedo*

I

I yo *yo*
ice hielo, el *eeyelo*
ice cream helados, los *elados*
  ice cream cornet cornete, el *korneteh*
  ice cream shop heladería, la
  eladereea
iced drink granizado, el *graneethado*
included incluido *inklweedo*
information información, la
  eenformatheeon
ink tinta, la *teenta*
inn mesón, el *meson*
insurance seguro, el *segooro*
interesting interesante *eenteresanteh*
interval descanso, el *deskanso*
iron plancha, la *plantcha*

J

jacket chaqueta, la *chaketa*
jam mermelada, la *mermelada*
jeans vaqueros, los *bakeros*
jeweller's joyería, la **choyereea*
juice zumo, el *thoomo*
jumper jersey, el/suéter, el **cherseh/
sweter*

K

kebab brocheta, la *brotcheta*
key llave, la *yabeh*
kidney riñón, el *reenyon*
king prawn langostino, el *langosteeno*
kiosk, newspaper stall quiosco de
  prensa, el *keeosko deh prensa*
knee rodilla, la *rodeeya*
knickers braga, la *braga*
to know saber *saber*

L

later luego *lwego*
laundry lavandería, la *labandereea*
laxative laxante, el *lasanteh*
leather cuero, el *kwero*
to leave salir *saleer*

leave me alone! ¡déjeme en paz!
  de*chemeh en path
leek puerro, el *pwerro*
left-hand side izquierda, la
  eethkeeyerda
leg pierna, la *peeyerna*
lemon limón, el *leemon*
lemonade gaseosa, la *gaseosa*
lentils lentejas, las *lente*chas*
letter carta, la *karta*
lettuce lechuga, la *lechooga*
life vida, la *beeda*
lift ascensor, el *asthensor*
lights luces, las *loothes*
  car lights luces del coche, las *loothes
  del kotcheh*
line línea, la *leenea*
little poco *poko*
to live vivir *beebeer*
liver hígado, el *eegado*
loaf of bread barra de pan, la *barra
deh pan*
lobster langosta, la *langosta*
loin (pork) lomo de cerdo *lomo deh
therdo*
to lose perder *perder*
lost perdido/a *perdeedo*

M

mackerel caballa, la *kabaya*
magazine revista, la *rebeesta*
magnificent magnífico/a
  magneefeekola
many muchos/as *mootchos/as*
map (town) plano, el *plano* (world)
  mapa, el *mapa*
marinated al adobo *al adobo*
market mercado, el *merkado*
marmalade mermelada de naranja, la
  mermelada deh naran*cha
marrow calabaza, la *kalabatha*
marzipan mazapán, el *mathapan*
match (football) partido, el *parteedo*
  (for lighting) cerilla, la *thereeya*
mayonnaise mahonesa, la *maeeonesa*
maze laberinto, el *labereento*
meat carne, la *karneh*
meatballs albóndigas, las *albondeegas*
medium (steak) a punto *a poonto*
melon melón, el *melon*
menu carta, la *karta*
metro (underground) metro, el *metro*
  metro card tarjeta de metro, la
  tar*cheta deh metro
midday mediodía, el *medeeodeea*
midnight medianoche, la
  medeeanotcheh
mileage kilometraje *keelometra*cheh*

milk leche, la *letcheh*
milk shake batido, el *bateedo*
minced meat picadillo, el *peekadeeyo*
mineral water (sparkling/still) agua
    mineral (con gas/sin gas), el *agwa
    meeneral (kon gas, seen gas)*
mistake error, el *error*
mixed mixto/a *meesto/a*
modern moderno/a *moderno/a*
money dinero, el *deenero*
month mes, el *mes*
monument monumento, el
    monoomento
more más *mas*
morning mañana *manyana*
motorbike moto, la *moto*
motorway autopista, la *owtopeesta*
mouth boca, la *boka*
to move mover *mober*
much mucho/a *mootcho/a*
museum museo, el *moosayo*
mushrooms champiñones, los
    champeenyones (wild) seta, la *seta*
music música, la *mooseeka*
mussels mejillones, los
    me*cheeyones
mustard mostaza, la *mostatha*

N

name nombre, el *nombreh*
    my name is me llamo *meh yamo*
napkin servilleta, la *serbeeyeta*
nappy pañal, el *panyal*
near (to) cerca (de) *therka (deh)*
nearby cercano/a *therkano*
neck cuello, el *kweyo*
necklace collar, el *koyar*
to need necesitar *netheseetar*
newspaper periódico *pereeodeeko*
next próximo/a *proseemo/a*
nice to meet you encantado/a
    enkantado/a
night noche, la *notcheh*
no no *no*
noodles fideos, los *feedeos*
nose nariz, la *nareeth*
nothing nada *nada*
nougat turrón, el *toorron*
now ahora *aora*
number número, el *noomero*
nurse enfermero/a *enfermero/a*
nut nuez, la *nooweth*

O

occupied ocupado/a *okoopado/a*
octopus pulpo, el *poolpo*
of de *deh*
of course claro *klaro*
oil aceite, el *athayeeteh*

okay? ¿todo bien? *todo beeyen*
old viejo/a *beeye*cho/a*
olive aceituna, la *athayeetoona*
omelette (Spanish) tortilla española,
    la *torteeya espanyola*
onion cebolla, la *theboya*
open abierto/a *abeeyerto/a*
to open abrir *abreer*
opera ópera, la *opera*
to operate operar *operar*
orange naranja, la *naran*cha*
    fizzy orange drink naranjada, la
    naran*chada
outskirts cercanías, las *therkaneeas*
oxtail rabo de buey, el *rabo deh
    bweh*
oysters ostras, las *ostras*

P

packet paquete, el *paketeh*
painting pintura, la *peentoora*
palace palacio, el *palatheeo*
pardon? ¿cómo? *komo*
park parque, el *parkeh*
to park (a car) aparcar *aparkar*
parsley perejil, el *pere*cheel*
partridge perdiz, la *perdeeth*
party fiesta, la *feeyesta*
passport pasaporte, el *pasaporteh*
pastries repostería, la *repostereea*
pastry bollo, el *boyo*
to pay pagar *pagar*
peach melocotón, el *melokoton*
peanuts cacahuetes, los *kakawetes*
pear pera, la *pera*
peas guisantes, los *geesantes*
people gente, la/personas, las
    *chenteh/personas
pepper (spice) pimienta, la
    peemeeyenta (vegetable) pimiento,
    el *peemeeyento*
person persona, la *persona*
petrol gasolina, la *gasoleena*
petrol gasolina, la *gasoleena*
    unleaded gasolina sin plomo, la
    gasoleena seen plomo
pheasant faisán, el *faeesan*
phone card tarjeta telefónica, la
    tar*cheta telefoneeka
pickled escabechado/a *eskabetchado*
pie tarta, la *tarta*
pig cerdo, el *therdo*
pill pastilla, la *pasteeya*
pillow almohada, la *almoada*
pine kernels piñones, los *peenyones*
pineapple piña, la *peenya*
pitcher jarra, la **charra*
plaster (sticking) tiritas, las *teereetas*

platform andén, el/vía, la *anden/bee*a
please por favor *por fabor*
plum ciruela, la *theeroowel*a
police policía, la *poleethee*a
police station comisaría, la
*komeesaree*a
pork cerdo, el *therd*o
port puerto, el *pwert*o
portion ración, la *rathee*on
post office correos *korray*os
postcard postal, la *postal*
potato patata, la *patat*a
mashed potatoes puré de patatas, el
*pooreh deh patat*as
poultry aves, las *ab*es
pound (£) libra, la *leebr*a
prawns gambas, las *gamb*as
pregnant embarazada *embarathad*a
prescription receta, la *rethet*a
to present presentar *present*ar
to press apretar *apret*ar
programme programa, el *program*a
pub taberna, la *tabern*a
puncture pinchazo, el *peentchath*o
purse monedero, el *moned*ero

Q

question pregunta, la *pregoon*ta
quick rápido/a *rapeed*o/a
quince/quince jelly membrillo, el
*membreey*o
quite bastante *bastant*eh

R

racket raqueta, la *raket*a
radish rábano, el *raban*o
railway ferrocarril, el *ferrokarreel*
railway station estación del ferrocarril,
la *estatheeon deh ferrocarreel*
raisin pasa, la *pas*a
rare (steak) poco hecho/a *poko
etch*o/a
raspberry frambuesa, la *frambwes*a
raw crudo/a *krood*o/a
ready listo/a *leest*o/a
receipt recibo, el *retheeb*o
to recommend recomendar *rekomend*ar
red rojo/a *ro***ch*o/a
red cabbage lombarda, la *lombard*a
red wine vino tinto, el *beeno teent*o
registration number (car) matrícula
*matreekool*a
to repeat repetir *repet*eer
reservation reserva, la *reserb*a
to rest descansar *deskans*ar
restaurant restaurante, el *restowrant*eh
return ticket billete de ida y vuelta
*beeyeteh deh eeda ee bwelt*a

rice arroz, el *arroth*
rice pudding arroz con leche, el
*arroth kon letch*eh
right away en seguida *en segeed*a
right-hand side derecha, la *deretch*a
ring anillo, el/sortija, la *aneey*o,
sortee**ch*a
river río, el *ree*o
road (residential) calle, la *kay*eh (main)
carretera, la *carret*era
roast asado/a *asad*o/a
roast beef rosbif, el *rosbeef*
roe huevas, las *web*as
roll (of film) carrete, el *karret*eh
room habitación, la *abeetathee*on
double room habitación doble, la
*abeetatheeon dob*leh
single room habitación individual, la
*abeetatheeon eendeebeedoo*al
rum ron, el *ron*
Russian ruso/a *roos*o/a

S

safe (for valuables) caja fuerte, la
ka**cha fwert*eh
sage salvia, la *salbee*a
sail vela, la *bel*a
salad ensalada, la *ensalad*a
salmon salmón, el *salmon*
salt sal, la *sal*
same mismo/a *meesm*o/a
sandwich bocadillo, el *bokadeey*o
sanitary towels compresas, los
*kompres*as
sardine sardina, la ·*sardeen*a
sausage salchicha, la *saltcheetch*a
spicy sausage chorizo, el/longaniza, la
*choreetho/longanee*ta
sautéed salteado/a *saltead*o/a
to say decir *deth*eer
scallop vieira, la *beeayr*a
scarf bufanda, la *boofand*a
sea bream besugo, el *besoog*o
seafood mariscos, los *mareesk*os
seafood restaurant marisquería, la
*mareeskeree*a
second segundo/a *segoond*o
to see ver *ber*
self-service autoservicio
*owtoserbeethe*o
separate aparte *apart*eh
serious grave *grab*eh
to serve servir *serb*eer
set dishes platos combinados, los
*platos kombeenad*os
set menu menú del día *menoo del dee*a
shandy clara, la *klar*a
shellfish mariscada, la *mareeskad*a

sherry jerez, el *chereth
  dry sherry fino, el *feeno*
shirt camisa, la *kameesa*
shoe zapato, el *thapato*
shoe shop zapatería, la *thapatereea*
shop tienda, la *teeyenda*
shoulder hombro, el *ombro*
show espectáculo, el *espektakoolo*
to show mostrar *mostrar*
shower ducha, la *dootcha*
shrimps camarones, los *kamarones*
sights monumentos, los *monoomentos*
to sign firmar *feermar*
simple sencillo/a *sentheeyo/a*
single (unmarried) soltero/a *soltero/a*
single ticket billete de ida, el *beeyeteh deh eeda*
size (clothes) talla, la *taya* (shoe) tamaño, el *tamanyo*
to ski esquiar *eskeear*
skiing esquí, el *eskee*
skirt falda, la *falda*
to sleep dormir *dormeer*
slowly despacio *despatheeo*
small pequeño/a *pekenyo/a*
smoked ahumado/a *aoomado/a*
smoking/non smoking fumador/no fumador *foomadoor, no foomador*
snacks tapas, las *tapas* (large portion) raciones, las *ratheeones*
snails caracoles de tierra, los *karakoles deh teeyerra*
socks calcetines, los *kaltheteenes*
sole (fish) lenguado, el *lengwado*
solution solución, la *solootheeon*
son hijo, el *ee*cho*
sorbet sorbete, el *sorbeteh*
sorry (excuse me) perdone *perdoneh* (I'm sorry) lo siento *lo seeyento*
soup sopa, la *sopa*
spaghetti espaguetis, los *espagetees*
Spanish español/a *espanyol*
sparkling espumoso *espoomoso*
to speak hablar *ablar*
speciality (local) plato típico, el *plato teepeeko*
spicy picante *peekanteh*
spinach espinacas, las *espeenakas*
spring primavera, la *preemabera*
square plaza, la *platha*
  main square plaza mayor, la *platha mayor*
squid calamares, los *kalamares*
stadium estadio, el *estadeeo*
staircase escalera, la *eskalera*
stalls (in theatre) platea, la *platea*

stamp sello, el *seyo*
starter (meal) entradas, las *entradas*
station estación, la *estatheeon*
stationer's shop papelería, la *papelereea*
to stay quedar *kedar*
steak entrecot, el *entrekot* (fillet) solomillo, el *solomeeyo*
steamed cocido al vapor *kotheedo al bapor*
stew cazuela, la/cocido, el/fabada, la *kathwela/kotheedo/fabada*
stewed estofado/a *estofado/a*
sting picadura, la *peekadoora*
stockings medias, las *medeeas*
to stop (finish) terminar *termeenar*
stop (train/bus etc.) parada, la *parada*
straight away ahora mismo *aora meesmo*
straight on todo recto *todo rekto*
strawberry fresa, la *fresa*
street calle, la *kayeh*
to stroll pasear *pasear*
to study estudiar *estoodeear*
stuffed relleno/a *reyeno/a*
subtitles subtítulos, los *soobteetoolos*
sugar azúcar, el *athookar*
to suit quedar *kedar*
  it suits you le queda bien *leh keda beeyen*
suitcase maleta, la *maleta*
summer verano, el *berano*
sunburn quemaduras de sol, las *kemadooras del sol*
sun shade sombrilla, la *sombreeya*
supermarket supermercado, el *soopermerkado*
surgery ambulatorio, el *amboolatoreeo*
surname apellido, el *apeyeedo*
sweet dulce *dooltheh*
sweetcorn maíz, el *maeeth*
swimming pool piscina, la *peestheena*
swordfish pez espada, el *peth espada*

T

tablecloth mantel, el *mantel*
tagliatelle tallarines, los *tayareenes*
to take (hold of) tomar *tomar*
to take out (tooth) sacar *sakar*
tap grifo, el *greefo*
tart tarta, la *tarta*
taxi taxi *tasi*
  taxi rank parada de taxis, la *parada deh tasees*

tea té, el *teh*
  camomile tea manzanilla, la *manthaneeya*
  herbal tea infusión, la *eenfooseeon*
  mint tea té de menta *teh deh menta*
telephone teléfono, el *telefono*
telephone box cabina, la *kabeena*
television televisión, la *telebeeseeon*
tennis court cancha de tenis, la *kantcha deh tenees*
tent tienda (de campaña), la *teeyenda (deh kampanya)*
thank you (muchas) gracias *mootchas gratheeas*
that ese/esa, aquél/aquella *eseh/esa, akel/akeya*
theatre teatro, el *teatro*
their su *soo*
then entonces *entonthes*
there allí *ayee*
there is, there are hay *aee*
these éstos/as *estos/as*
thigh muslo, el *mooslo*
to think pensar *pensar* (to believe) creer *kreyer*
third tercero/a *terthero/a*
this este/esta *esteh/a*
those esos/as, aquellos/aquellas *esos/ esas, akeyos/akeyas*
throat garganta, la *garganta*
thumb pulgar, el *poolgar*
ticket (for show etc.) entrada, la *entrada* (travel) billete, el *beeyeteh*
ticket office taquilla, la *takeeya*
tie corbata, la *korbata*
tights medias, las *medeeas*
tile azulejo, el *athoole*cho*
time tiempo, el *teeyempo*
timetable horario, el *orareeo*
tip propina, la *propeena*
toast pan tostado, el *pan tostado*
tobacconist's estanco, el *estanko*
today hoy *oy*
toilet lavabo, el/servicios, los/aseos, los *lababo, serbeetheeos, aseos*
toilet paper papel higiénico, el *papel ee*cheeyeneeko*
toll peaje, el *peya*cheh*
tomato tomate, el *tomateh*
tomorrow mañana *manyana*
tongue lengua, la *lengwa*
tonic water tónica, la *toneeka*
tooth muela, la *mwela*
toothpick palillo de dientes, el *paleeyo deh deeyentes*
tourist office oficina de turismo, la *ofeetheena deh tooreesmo*

towel toalla, la *toaya*
town hall ayuntamiento, el *aeeoontameeyento*
toy juguete, el **choogeteh*
train tren, el *tren*
train (high-speed) AVE *abeh*
traveller's cheque cheque de viaje, el *chekeh deh beea*cheh*
trip viaje, el *beea*cheh* (day trip) excursión, la *eskoortheeon*
tripe callos, los *kayos*
trousers pantalón, el *pantalon*
trout trucha, la *trootcha*
trunks (swimming) bañador, el *banyador*
to try on probar *probar*
T-shirt camiseta, la *kameeseta*
tuna atún, el/bonito, el *atoon, boneeto*
turbot rodaballo, el *rodabayo*
turkey pavo, el *pabo*
turnip nabo, el *nabo*

U

underpants calzoncillo, el *kalthontheeyo*
to understand entender *entender*
unlimited ilimitado *eeleemeetado*
urgent urgente *oor*chenteh*

V

vanilla vainilla, la *baeeneeya*
veal ternera, la *ternera*
vegetables verduras, las *berdooras*
vegetarian vegetariano/a *be*chetereeano*
venison venado, el *benado*
vermouth vermú *bermoo*
vest camiseta, la *kameeseta*
viewpoint mirador, el *meerador*
vinegar vinagre, el *beenagreh*
to vomit vomitar *bomeetar*

W

wafer (ice cream) barquillo, el *barkeeyo*
waiter/waitress camarero/a *kamarero*
wallet cartera, la *kartera*
walls (town) muralla, la *mooraya*
to want querer *kerer*
watch reloj, el *relo*ch*
watchmaker's relojería, la *relo*chereea*
watch out! ¡cuidado! *kweedado*
water agua, la *agwa*
watermelon sandía, la *sandeea*
waterskiing esquí acuático, el *eskee akwateeko*
to wear llevar *yebar*
week semana, la *semana*

weekend fin de semana, el *feen deh semana*
well done (steak) bien hecho/a *beeyen etcho/a*
what? ¿qué? *keh*
  what time is it? ¿qué hora es? *keh ora es*
whelks caracoles de mar, los *karakoles deh mar*
where? ¿dónde? *dondeh*
white blanco/a *blanko/a*
whiting pescadilla, la *peskadeeya*
wife esposa, la *esposa*
windsurf board plancha, la *plantcha*
wine vino, el *beeno*
  red wine vino tinto, el *beeno teento*
  rosé vino rosado, el *beeno rosado*
  white wine vino blanco, el *beeno blanko*
wine cellar bodega, la *bodega*
winter invierno, el *eenbeeyerno*
without sin *seen*
wool lana, la *lana*
to work (job) trabajar *traba*char*
  (function) funcionar *foontheeonar*
to worry preocuparse *preokooparseh*
to write escribir *eskreebeer*

Y

yellow amarillo/a *amareeyo/a*
yes sí *see*
yesterday ayer *aeeyer*
yoghurt yogur, el *yogoor*
you tú, usted *too, oosteth*
your su *soo*

A

a to
abrigo, el coat
abrir to open
acceso access
aceite, el oil
aceituna, la olive
aceptar to take/accept
adiós goodbye
adulto/a adult
aeropuerto, el airport
aftersun, el after-sun lotion
agencia, la agency
agotado/a sold out
agua, el water
agua mineral (con gas/sin gas), el mineral water (sparkling/still)
aguacate, el avocado
aguardiente, el spirit
ahora now
ahora mismo straight away
ahumado/a smoked
aire, el air
aire acondicionado, el air conditioning
ajo, el garlic
al adobo marinated
al horno in the oven/baked
albaricoque, el apricot
albóndigas, las meatballs
alcachofa, la artichoke
alérgico/a allergic
¿algo más? anything else?
algodón, el cotton
alimentación, la groceries
allí there
almeja, la clam
almendra, la almond
almohada, la pillow
alpinismo, el climbing
alquilar to hire
alubias blancas, las butter beans
alubias pintas, las red kidney beans
alubias, las beans
amarillo/a yellow
ambiente, el environment
ambulancia, la ambulance
ambulatorio, el doctor's surgery
andén, el platform
anfiteatro, el circle (in theatre)
angulas, las baby eels
anillo, el ring
anís, el anis
anteayer the day before yesterday
antibióticos, los antibiotics
antihistamínico, el antihistamine
aparcar to park

apartamento, el apartment, flat
aparte separate
aperitivo, el aperitif
apio, el celery
aplicar to apply
aplíquese put on/apply
aprétar to press
aquél that one
aquí here
aquí tiene here you are
arenque, el herring
arroz, el rice
arroz blanco, el boiled rice
arroz con leche, el rice pudding
asado/a roasted
asado con espetón roasted on the spit
ascensor, el lift
aseos, los toilets/cloakroom
asma, el asthma
aspirina, la aspirin
atún, el tuna
autobús, el bus
autocar, el coach
autopista, la motorway
autoservicio, el self-service
autovía, la A-road
avellana, la hazelnut
avería, la breakdown
aves, las poultry
ayer yesterday
ayuntamiento, el town hall
azúcar, el sugar
azul blue
azulejo, el tile

B

bacalao, el cod(fish)
bailar to dance
balcón, el balcony
bañador, el swimming trunks
banco, el bank
baño, el bathroom
barato cheap
barca, la boat
barquillo, el ice-cream wafer
barra de pan, la loaf of bread
barrio, el town district
bastante lejos a fairly long way away
batería, la battery
batido, el milk shake
beber to drink
bebida, la drink
berenjena, la aubergine
berza, la cabbage
besugo, el sea bream
bicicleta, la bike
bien hecho/a well done (steak)
billete de ida y vuelta return ticket

billete de ida, el single ticket
billete, el ticket
bistec, el grilled steak
bizcocho, el sponge biscuit
blanco/a white
blusa, la blouse
boca, la mouth
bocadillo, el sandwich
bodega, la traditional bar
bollo, el bun
bolsa, la bag
bolso, el handbag
bonito, el tuna
boquerón, el anchovy
bota, la boot
botella, la bottle
botón, el button
braga, la knickers
brasa, la barbecue
brazo, el arm
brocheta, la skewer, kebab
brócoli, el broccoli
buenas noches good night
buenas tardes good afternoon/
  evening
bueno/a good
buenos días good morning
bufanda, la scarf
buñuelo, el doughnut

C

caballa, la mackerel
caballeros, los gentlemen
cabeza, la head
cabina, la telephone box
cabrito, el kid (baby goat)
cacahuetes, los peanuts
cacerola, la casserole
cadera, la hip
café, el coffee
café con hielo, el iced coffee
café con leche, el creamy white
  coffee
café cortado, el slightly white coffee
café descafeinado, el decaffeinated
  coffee
café irlandés Irish coffee
café solo, el black coffee
caja de tiritas, la sticking plaster
caja fuerte, la safe
calabacín, el courgette
calabaza, la marrow
calamar, el squid
calcetines, los socks
caldo, el clear soup
caliente hot
calle, la street
callos, los tripe

calzoncillo, el underpants
cama, la bed
cama de niño, la child's bed
cama individual, la single bed
cama de matrimonio, la double bed
camarero/a waiter/waitress
camarones, los shrimps
cambiar to change (money)
camisa, la shirt
camiseta, la vest/T-shirt
camping, el campsite
campo de golf, el golf course
caña, la draught beer
cancha de tenis, la tennis court
canelones, los cannelloni
cangrejo, el crab
caracoles de mar, los whelks
caracoles de tierra, los snails
caravana, la caravan
carnaval, el carnival
carne, la meat
carne de vaca, la beef
carnicería, la butcher's (shop)
carrete, el roll (of film)
carretera, la (main) road
carta, la letter/menu
cartera, la wallet
casa de huéspedes, la bed and
  breakfast
casco viejo, el old town
castaña, la chestnut
castillo, el castle
catedral, la cathedral
cava, el sparkling wine
caza, la game (food)
cazuela, la stew
cebolla, la onion
cena, la dinner
cenicero, el ashtray
centro (ciudad), el (town) centre
cerámica, la ceramics
cercanías, las outskirts/suburbs
cercano/a near
cerdo, el pig
cereza, la cherry
cerrado closed
cerrar to close
cervecería, la bar/pub
cerveza, la bottled beer
champán, el champagne
champiñones, los mushrooms
chaqueta, la jacket
charcutería, la delicatessen
charlar to chat
cheque de viaje, el traveller's cheque
chirimoya, la custard apple
chocolate, el chocolate
chorizo, el spicy sausage

chuleta, la chop, cutlet
churros, los fritters
cigarrillo, el cigarette
cine, el cinema
cinta, la cassette
cinturón, el belt
ciruela, la plum
clara, la shandy
claro of course
coche, el car
coche de alquiler, el hire car
cocido, el stew
cocido/a boiled/stewed
cocido al vapor steamed
codo, el shoulder
col, la cabbage
colega, el/la colleague
coliflor, la cauliflower
collar, el necklace
comercio, el store
comestibles, los groceries
comisaría, la police station
comisión, la commission charge
¿cómo? pardon?
completo/a full
comprar to buy
compresas, los sanitary towels
con guía guided tour
coñac, el brandy
concierto, el concert
condón, el condom
constipado/a to have a cold
copa, la wine glass
copita, la sherry glass
corbata, la tie
cornete, el ice-cream cornet
correos post office
corrida de toros, la bullfight
cortado/a cut
creer to think/believe
crema, la cream/custard
creo I think/believe
croqueta, la croquette
cruce, el cross
crudo/a raw
cruzar to cross
cuajada, la junket
¿cuánto? how much?
¿cuánto son? how much are they?
¿cuánto tarda? how long does it take?
cubo de la basura, el dustbin
cubalibre, el white rum and coke
cubierto, el cover charge
cuello, el neck
cuenta, la bill
cuero, el leather
cuerpo, el body
¡cuidado! watch out!

D

dar to give
de of/from
decir to say
dedo, el finger
¡déjeme en paz! leave me alone!
dentista, el dentist
derecha, la right hand side
desayuno, el breakfast
descansar to rest
descanso, el interval
despacio slowly
día, el day
diabético/a diabetic
diarrea, la diarrhoea
dinero, el money
discoteca, la disco/nightclub
docena, la dozen
doler to hurt
dolor de cabeza, el headache
¿dónde? where?
¿dónde están? where are they?
dormir to sleep
ducha, la shower
duele it hurts
dulce sweet

E

embarazada pregnant
embutido, el sausage
empanadilla (de carne/pescado), la
  small (meat/fish) pasty
empanado/a breaded and fried
empastar to fill (a tooth)
en escabeche marinated
en seguida right away
en total all together
encantado/a nice to meet you
endivias, las chicory
enfermero/a nurse
ensalada, la salad
ensalada mixta, la mixed salad
ensaladilla rusa, la Russian salad
¿entiende? do you understand?
entonces then
entrada, la ticket/entrance
entradas, las starters
entrecot, el steak
entremeses, los hors d'oeuvres
error, el mistake
escabechado/a pickled
escalera, la staircase
escarola, la endive
escribir to write
ese/a that
esos/as those
espaguetis, los spaghetti
espalda, la back

español/a Spanish
espárragos, los asparagus
espectáculo, el show
espinacas, las spinach
esposa, la wife
espumoso sparkling wine
esquí, el skiing
esquí acuático, el water skiing
esquiar to ski
esquina, la corner
estación, la station
estación de autobuses, la bus station
estación del ferrocarril, la railway station
estadio, el stadium
estanco, el tobacconists
estar to be
éste this one
estofado stewed
estreñido/a to be constipated
estudiar to study
estudio I study
excursiones, las excursion
exposición, la exhibition
extranjero, el abroad

F

fabada, la white bean stew
faisán, el pheasant
falda, la skirt
farmacia de guardia, la emergency chemists
farmacia, la chemist's
feria, la festival/fair
ferretería, la hardware store
ferrocarril, el railway
fiambres, los cold meats
ficha, la form
fideos, los noodles
fiebre, la fever
fiesta, la party
filete, el fillet
fin de semana, el weekend
final, el end
fino, el dry sherry
firmar to sign
flan, el crème caramel
frambuesa, la raspberry
fresa, la strawberry
fresco/a fresh
frio/a cold
frito/a fried
frutería, la fruiterer's shop
fuegos artificiales, los fireworks
(no) fumador (non) smoking
funcionar to work/function
fútbol, el football

G

galería de arte, la art gallery
'gallinero', el 'gods' in theatre
gallina, la hen
gamba, la prawn
ganso, el goose
garbanzos, los chickpeas
garganta, la throat
garrafa, la carafe
gaseosa, la lemonade
gasolina, la petrol
gasolina sin plomo, la unleaded petrol
ginebra, la gin
gintonic, el gin and tonic
gracias thank you
grande big
granizado, el iced drink
gratuito/a free
grave serious
grifo, el tap
guantes, los gloves
guardarropa, el cloakroom
guía, la guide
guindilla, la chilli
guisantes, los peas
gusto, el taste/choice

H

habas, las broad beans
habichuelas, las haricot beans
habitación, la room
habitación doble, la double room
habitación individual, la single room
hablar to speak
hablo I speak
hay there is, there are
heladería, la ice-cream shop
helados, los ice-cream
hervido/a boiled
hielo, el ice
hierbas, las herbs
hígado, el liver
higo, el fig
hijo/a son/daughter
hinojo, el fennel
¡hola! hello!
hora, la hour
horario, el timetable
horchata, la milky, nut-based drink
hostal, el small hotel
hotel, el hotel
hoy today
hueso, el bone
huevas, las fish eggs/roe
huevos eggs
huevos cocidos/duros, los hard boiled eggs
huevos escalfados, los poached eggs

huevos pasados por agua, los boiled eggs
huevos revueltos, los scrambled eggs
huevos, los eggs

I

iglesia, la church
ilimitado unlimited
impresión, la printing
impresora, la printer
incluido included
información, la information
informática, la IT
infusión, la herbal tea
inglés/inglesa English
interesante interesting
invierno, el winter
izquierda, la left hand side

J

jabalí, el wild boar
jamón, el ham
jamón de York, el boiled ham
jamón serrano, el cured ham
jarabe, el cough mixture
jarra, la pitcher
jerez, el sherry
jersey, el jumper
joyería, la jeweller's
judías blancas, las haricot beans
judías verdes, las green/French beans
judías, las beans
juguete, el toy

K

kilometraje ilimitado unlimited mileage

L

laberinto, el maze
lana, la wool
langosta, la lobster
langostino, el king prawn
lavabo, el toilet
lavandería, la laundry
laxante, el laxative
le va bien it suits you
leche, la milk
lechuga, la lettuce
lejos a long way away
lengua, la tongue
lenguado, el sole (fish)
lentejas, las lentils
lentillas, las contact lenses
levantarse to get up
libra, la pound (£)
libre free
libro de reclamaciones, el complaint book (in hotel)
libro, el book
liebre, la hare

limón, el lemon
limonada, la fizzy lemon drink
línea, la line
listo/a ready
llave, la key
llegar to arrive
llénelo de fill up with
llevar to wear
lo siento I'm sorry
lo/la tomamos we'll take it
lombarda, la red cabbage
lomo de cerdo, el pork loin (pieces)
longaniza, la spicy sausage
luces (del coche), las (car) lights
luego later

M

magdalena, la fairy cake
magnífico/a magnificent
mahonesa, la mayonnaise
maíz, el sweetcorn
maleta, la suitcase
maletín, el briefcase
mañana tomorrow/morning
mano, la hand
manta, la blanket
mantel, el tablecloth
mantequilla, la butter
manzana, la apple
manzanilla, la camomile tea
mapa, el map
marido, el husband
mariscada, la mixed shellfish
mariscos, los seafood
marisquería, la seafood restaurant
marrón brown
más more
más o menos more or less/about
matrícula de coche, la car registration number
mazapán, el marzipan
me gusta (n) I like it/them
me llamo my name is
me lo/la llevo I'll take it
¿me puede ayudar? can you help me?
media hora, la half an hour
media pensión, la half board
medianoche, la midnight
medias, las stockings/tights
médico/a doctor
mediodía, el midday
mejillones, los mussels
melocotón, el peach
melón, el melon
membrillo, el quince/quince jelly
menú del día, el set lunch/dinner
mercadillo, el flea market
mercado, el market

merienda, la afternoon snack
merluza, la hake
mermelada, la jam
mermelada de naranja, la marmalade
mes, el month
mesón, el inn/pub
dinero en metálico, el cash
miel, la honey
minusválido/a invalid
mirador, el viewpoint
mismo/a the same
mitad de precio, la half price
mixto/a mixed
moda, la fashion
moderno/a modern
monedero, el purse
monumento, el monument
monumentos, los sights
moras, las blackberries
morcilla, la black pudding
mostaza, la mustard
moto, la motorbike
motor, el engine
mover to move
muchas gracias thank you very much
mucho/a much
muchos/as many
muela, la tooth
muralla, la walls of a town
museo, el museum
música, la music
muslo, el thigh

N

nabo, el turnip
nada nothing
  de nada don't mention it
naranja, la orange (fruit)
naranja orange (colour)
naranjada, la fizzy orange drink
nariz, la nose
nata, la cream
natillas, las egg custard
natural fresh/raw
negocio, el business
negro/a black
niño/a child
no no
no entiendo I don't understand
no hay we don't have any
no sé I don't know
no se preocupe don't worry
noche, la night
nombre, el name
nueces, las nuts
nuez, la nut
número, el number

O

ocupado/a taken/occupied
oficina de turismo, la tourist office
oído, el ear
¡oiga! excuse me/hello there!
ojos, los eyes
ópera, la opera
operar to operate
oreja, la outer ear
ostras, las oysters
otoño, el autumn

P

paella, la rice dish
pagar to pay
país, el country
palacio, el palace
palillo de dientes, el toothpick
palo de golf, el golf club
pan, el bread
pan tostado, el toast
pañal, el nappy
panceta, la bacon
pantalón, el trousers
papel higiénico, el toilet paper
papelería, la stationer's shop
paquete, el packet
para for
parada, la stop (train/bus etc.)
parada de taxis, la taxi rank
parador, el state-run hotel
parque, el park
parrillada, la mixed grill
partido de fútbol, el football match
pasa, la raisin
pasado mañana the day after
  tomorrow
pasaporte, el passport
pasear to stroll
pastel, el cake
pastelería, la cake shop
pastilla, la pill
patata, la potato
patatas fritas, las crisps, chips
pato, el duck
pavo, el turkey
peaje, el toll
pecho, el chest
película, la (en blanco y negro) (black and white) film (cinema or camera)
película en color, la colour film
pelota, la ball
pendientes, los earrings
pensión, la boarding house
pensión completa, la full board
pepinillo, el gherkin
pepino, el cucumber
pequeño/a small

pera, la pear
perder to lose
perdido/a lost
perdiz, la partridge
perdone excuse me
perejil, el parsley
periódicos extranjeros, los foreign
  newspapers
permiso de conducir, el driving licence
pero but
persiana, la blind
persona/as, la/s person/people
pescadilla, la whiting
pescaditos, los fried small fish
pescado, el fish
pescar to fish
pez espada, el swordfish
picadillo, el minced meat/sausage
picadura, la (insect) bite/sting
picante spicy
picatostes, los croutons
piel, la leather
pierna, la leg
pies, los feet
pila, la battery
pimentón (picante), el paprika
pimienta, la pepper (spice)
pimiento, el pepper (vegetable)
piña, la pineapple
pinchazo, el flat tyre
pincho moruno, el marinated pork
  kebab
piñones, los pine kernels
pintura, la painting
piscina, la swimming pool
plancha, la iron
plancha de windsurf, la windsurf board
plano, el plan
planta baja, la first floor
piso, la floor
plátano, el banana
platea, la stalls (in theatre)
plato del día, el dish of the day
plato típico de aquí, el local speciality
plato, el course (of meal)
platos combinados, los set dishes
playa, la beach
plaza mayor, la main square
plaza, la square
poco little
poco hecho/a rare/underdone (steak)
poder can, be able to
policía, la police
poliéster, el polyester
pollo, el chicken
pomelo, el grapefruit
póngame I'll have
pónganos we'll have

por for
por aquí this way
por favor please
postal, la postcard
postre, el sweet/dessert
preocuparse to worry
presentar to present
primavera, la spring
primero/a first
programa, el theatre programme
propina, la tip
próxima parada, la next stop
¿Puedo probármelo/la? can I try it on?
puente, el bridge
puerro, el leek
puerto, el port
pulgar, el thumb
pulpo, el octopus
pulsera, la bracelet
puré de patatas, el mashed potatoes
puro, el cigar

Q
¿Qué desea? what would you like?
¿Qué hora es? what time is it?
¿Qué le pasa? what's the matter?
¿Qué talla? what size?
¿Qué tipo? what type?
quedar to stay
quemaduras del sol, las sunburn
querer to want
queso, el cheese
queso fresco, el curd cheese
quiero I want/I'd like
quiosco de prensa, el kiosk

R
rábano, el radish
rabo de buey, el oxtail
ración, la portion
raciones, las bigger version of tapas
rape, el angler fish
rápido fast/quick
raqueta, la racket
raya, la skate (fish)
rebozado/a battered, breaded and fried
receta, la prescription
recibo, el receipt
recomendar to recommend
refresco, el cold drink
rehogado/a sautéed
rellenar to fill in
relleno stuffed
reloj, el watch
relojería, la watchmaker's
remolacha, la beetroot
repetir to repeat
repollo, el cabbage
repostería, la pastries